DESTINY OF PSYCHOLOGY

THE INNER WORLD THAT SHAPES US
WHERE IT REALLY BEGINS

TANMAY NAVNEET BITHRA

STRING PRODUCTION

Publisher:
STRING PRODUCTION
2H, 1066, Preet Vihar Colony,
Roorkee, Uttarakhand – 247667
Email: stringproductionofficial@gmail.com

DESTINY OF PSYCHOLOGY

ISBN: 978-93-6048-173-5

Cover Design & Book Layout by **Divyansh Manral**

Printed in India

Your life begins long before you understand it. Long before you learn to speak, long before you learn to defend yourself, and long before you learn what the world expects from you. It begins quietly, in rooms you barely remember, shaped by voices you did not choose and experiences you did not ask for. You open your eyes to a world that is already moving, already full of currents, already full of meanings that slowly settle inside you without your permission. People often talk about destiny as if it is a story written somewhere far away, but most of what shapes you begins inside the softest moments, the ones nobody sees, the ones you forget, but which never forget you.

There is something profoundly human about the way memories are carried without words. A child doesn't understand the world, yet somehow absorbs everything about it. A simple smile becomes safety. A loud tone becomes warning. A gentle touch becomes trust. A long silence becomes uncertainty. These small impressions enter the mind like whispers, but over time, they turn into the quiet rules a person subconsciously follows. You grow up believing you are choosing your reactions, yet many of them were chosen for you long before you noticed you were reacting at all.

Imagine a child standing near a window, watching raindrops slide down the glass. No one remembers this moment except the child. Maybe the room behind them is filled with noise, or maybe it is heavy with silence. The child doesn't know the meaning of the atmosphere, but they feel it. Every moment of warmth or fear settles into the inner foundation. Years later, as an adult, they may not recall that rainy afternoon, but the emotional residue of their early world continues to shape how they carry themselves.

Destiny begins quietly in this way. Not as a force outside you, but as a mood inside you. A feeling that grows from repeated experiences, repeated reactions, repeated patterns. The most powerful parts of your early identity are formed before you even know you have one.

People often believe they fully know themselves, yet most only know the outer layer — the version built from names, achievements, and roles. Beneath that lies a deeper identity formed from the smallest emotional imprints. You don't see this layer in the mirror, but you feel it in the way you respond to life. It shows up in the way you trust, the way you hesitate, the way you attach to others, and the way you pull away. It influences which opportunities feel possible to you, and which ones feel unreachable even when they are within your capacity.

Think of someone who hesitates before speaking in a group. They may believe they are simply "shy," yet their hesitation may come from a childhood where speaking up often led to criticism. They no longer remember the exact moments, but the feeling remains. Another person may boldly step into challenges because they grew up hearing encouragement. Nothing about their environment was perfect, yet they absorbed enough strength to continue taking steps forward. In both cases, destiny grows from patterns repeated long before adulthood begins.

The early years have a strange way of lingering. What you heard becomes what you believe. What you felt becomes what you expect. What you lacked becomes what you unconsciously seek. What hurt you becomes what you unknowingly fear repeating. People often underestimate how deeply a child's world stays alive within the adult they become.

There is a story I once heard about a boy growing up in a small, busy home filled with laughter, chaos, and unpredictability. He often sat on the floor with his toys while his mother cooked and his father shouted instructions from another room. One evening, during a storm, the power went out. The boy felt lost in the darkness until his mother lit a candle and placed it beside him. He remembers none of the conversations that happened that night. He doesn't remember the food or the noise or the arguments. What stayed with him was the tiny circle of warm light that made him feel safe. That simple moment influenced something inside him. Even as an adult, he always placed a small lamp at his bedside, not for lighting, but for comfort. Some feelings remain long after the memories fade.

That is how destiny begins — with impressions that linger quietly, shaping your perception without your awareness.

You grow older and begin to believe that life is shaped by big decisions, grand opportunities, or dramatic turning points. Yet when you look closely at your own story, you begin to notice that the turning points were rarely dramatic. They were often small shifts in how you felt, what you believed, or how you interpreted a moment. People imagine that transformation is sudden, but in reality, it grows the way morning light fills a room — slowly, gently, almost unnoticeably, until eventually everything looks clearer.

A person may spend years repeating the same patterns without knowing why. They may find themselves drawn to similar friendships, similar mistakes, similar emotional roads. Nothing feels new because the inner map hasn't changed. The inner world continues to recreate familiar situations, not because the person wants them, but because the mind repeats what it knows. Familiarity feels safe, even when it hurts. It is easier to follow an old script than to write a new one, especially if the script was written long before adulthood.

Yet within every person, there is also a deeper self — the part that sees beyond habits, beyond fear, beyond old influences. This part does not shout. It appears in small moments of clarity: a sudden silence in the middle of a busy day, a feeling that something must change, a quiet knowing that you are meant for more than your patterns suggest. Some call this intuition, some call it inner truth, but regardless of the name, it is the one part of you untouched by early shaping. It is the self that existed before the world told you who you were supposed to be.

When this deeper self stirs, it often creates tension with the outer self. You may feel restless without knowing why. You may feel drawn toward something unknown, or disconnected from routines that once felt normal. This tension is not weakness; it is a sign that the path inside you is shifting. It signals the beginning of awareness — the moment you realize that your life is not just a result of what happened to you, but also of what you choose to understand about yourself.

There is a woman who once said that she spent her life trying to be agreeable because she learned early on that peace depended on her silence. She was praised for being “easy,” “quiet,” and “well-behaved.” As an adult, she struggled to express her true feelings. It wasn’t until she sat one day, alone with her thoughts, that she realized her entire personality had been built around preventing conflict. This moment of recognition didn't change her overnight, but it changed the way she saw her past. Understanding became the first step toward choosing something new. Her destiny began shifting from that moment of awareness.

Awareness is like turning on a light in a room you have been sitting in for years. The room has always been the same, but you finally see where everything is placed.

Life may not always feel like it is in your control. The world around you can be unpredictable, unfair, or overwhelming. But the inner world — the place where your interpretations live — becomes your compass. When you understand what shaped you, you begin to understand what directs you. You begin to see the difference between who you are and who you became because of circumstances.

Destiny does not come from a single moment that defines everything. It comes from countless moments that slowly shape your sense of self. Some are gentle, some are painful, some are confusing, and some are enlightening. Each moment becomes a thread in a larger pattern. And when you finally step back and observe that pattern, you begin to understand the story you've been living.

Part of being human is realizing that every experience, even the ones you wish you could forget, becomes part of the deeper mosaic of your life. Some pieces add strength, some add vulnerability, some add caution, and some add hope. None exist alone; they connect to form the person you are right now.

Destiny is not written outside you. It grows quietly inside you through every moment that touched you deeply, even when you didn't recognize its importance at the time.

THE PATTERNS WE CARRY FORWARD

Life has a way of shaping you even when you are completely unaware of it. You grow older, and with age comes the illusion that you are now fully responsible for the direction you take. Yet so much of what feels like your "choice" is quietly influenced by experiences you barely remember. You notice certain feelings rise in familiar situations, and you may wonder, "Why do I react like this?" That question is not a sign of confusion. It is the beginning of understanding.

There is an invisible thread connecting the person you were as a child to the person you are today. This thread does not pull you backward, but it does remind you of who you learned to be. Some people grow up in environments where encouragement was rare, so they step into adulthood doubting their abilities long before they even try. Others grow up surrounded by warmth, so they enter the world trusting more easily, believing that challenges can be overcome. Neither path is fixed, but both paths influence the starting point.

A memory can live inside a person long after it has been forgotten. A moment of embarrassment in school may make someone fear speaking years later. A single look of disappointment from a parent can become the seed of a lifelong need to prove oneself. A moment of unexpected kindness can become the first place where hope quietly settles. These memories—whether loud or silent—leave traces that grow into patterns. And these patterns eventually become the inner lens through which a person interprets life.

There was once a young girl named Mira. She grew up in a home where silence was more common than conversation. Her parents were kind, but quiet, and rarely expressed emotion openly. Mira learned to read their moods from their eyes rather than their words. She grew up believing that expressing herself might trouble others. Years later, as an adult, she often struggled to say what she truly felt. Even in moments where she wanted to speak, something inside her held back. She wasn't being shy; she was following the emotional script her childhood gave her. Her destiny, in that sense, began long before she knew the meaning of the word.

Yet the remarkable thing about people is that the inner script is never unchangeable. One evening, Mira met a friend who asked her a simple question: "What do you want?" She expected herself to answer easily, but she couldn't. The silence she knew so well from her childhood rose again, but this time she noticed it. That moment—quiet, almost invisible—became the first time she realized her voice had been waiting inside her all along. It took years of living silently for her to understand that she had something to say. Awareness didn't erase her past, but it helped her see where her reactions came from. And that clarity became her turning point.

This is how people change. Not through sudden transformations, but through noticing. Life continues to unfold on the outside, but the inner world slowly shifts as you begin to understand yourself more deeply. Some people spend years thinking something is wrong with them, when in reality, they are simply carrying patterns formed in environments that no longer match their life today.

Your inner world is not only shaped by childhood. Every stage of life adds something. Friendships leave marks. Disappointments reshape expectations. Mistakes create caution. Unexpected kindness builds trust. Even moments of loneliness contribute to the way a person learns to stand on their own feet. Each experience—tiny or big—adds another layer to your understanding of yourself.

Think of a moment when you felt misunderstood. Perhaps you tried to explain your thoughts, but the words wouldn't form. Or perhaps someone reacted in a way you didn't expect. These moments linger because they echo something deeper inside you. People carry emotional echoes from their past, and these echoes influence how they interpret the present.

There was a man named arjun who grew up feeling responsible for everyone around him. Whenever someone in his family suffered, he rushed to fix it. As an adult, he still felt that same urgency. Whenever a friend was upset, he believed it was his responsibility to make things better. He never questioned why he felt burdened by others 'emotions, but the truth was simple: he learned early in life that love meant carrying weight. It wasn't until he experienced a situation he couldn't fix that he realized something important—he was tired, not because he didn't care, but because he cared too much. And caring too much was something he learned long before he understood he had a choice.

The inner world often becomes clearer in moments of exhaustion than in moments of success. When you reach a point where your usual patterns stop working, your mind begins to reveal the deeper layers you once overlooked. Many people discover their true selves during quiet moments of reflection rather than during achievements. Achievements excite you for a while, but reflection transforms you softly, quietly, in ways you may not even notice until much later.

Destiny cannot be understood if you only look at the big events of your life. You have to look at the subtle ones—the way your chest tightens before making a decision, the ease with which you trust or the hesitation with which you step forward, the emotions that rise when you feel ignored, the pull you feel toward certain dreams, the discomfort that appears when you step outside old patterns. None of these reactions happen by accident. They grow from your inner story.

Every person carries an unspoken "why" behind their habits. Someone becomes perfectionistic because they learned that mistakes brought disapproval. Another becomes carefree because structure once felt suffocating. Someone else develops a habit of overthinking because uncertainty once led to pain. And another becomes very decisive because they once lived in a world where waiting meant losing opportunities.

These tendencies are not flaws. They are survival shapes—forms your inner self adopted to move through earlier chapters of life. They helped you then. They may limit you now. But the moment you understand their origin, they lose their power to control your path from the shadows.

Life has a rhythm that slowly teaches you about yourself. You learn through contrast—through days that feel aligned and days that feel disconnected. When something feels right, it usually matches your inner nature. When something consistently feels wrong, it often contradicts who you truly are. That discomfort is not a mistake; it is information. It is the inner self trying to tell you that a certain path does not belong to you.

There is a young man named Imran who spent years following a path chosen by his family. He excelled in everything he tried, yet felt strangely hollow. Everyone admired him, but he felt unseen. He completed tasks flawlessly, yet felt disconnected from meaning. Nothing was wrong on the outside, but everything felt slightly off inside him. One day, while walking home from a long day of routine, he paused in the middle of the street and realized something startling: he couldn't remember the last time he felt genuinely alive. It wasn't sadness he felt; it was absence. And that absence revealed the truth—his life was moving, but he wasn't moving with it.

This is how many destinies drift quietly. Not through major failures, but through subtle misalignment. You live the life expected of you, but not the one that resonates with your inner self. You succeed by every external measure, yet feel a faint emptiness that grows louder with time. This is not failure. This is the mind's way of reminding you that your path is meant to be shaped from the inside, not by the demands of the world around you.

Understanding destiny is not about predicting what will happen. It is about recognizing the forces already guiding you from within. When you understand your patterns, you understand your direction. When you understand your emotional roots, you understand your reactions. When you understand the quiet signals inside you, you understand the difference between what feels forced and what feels natural.

The inner world is always speaking, but it uses a language of feelings, not words. A feeling of heaviness may mean a path is not yours. A sense of calm may mean you are stepping where you were meant to step. A spark of excitement may reveal a hidden truth about your desires. And hesitation may point to old fear rather than genuine caution.

Destiny begins to reveal itself when you stop ignoring the small shifts inside you.

Part of becoming aware of your inner world is learning to recognize what belongs to you and what was handed to you. Not all of your fears are your own. Not all of your beliefs began with you. Not all of your habits were chosen consciously. Some came from years of watching, listening, absorbing, and adapting. And yet, despite carrying so much from the past, every person reaches a moment where they pause and begin asking the questions that truly matter: "Who am I beyond what shaped me? What lives beneath my patterns? What part of me has been waiting to be understood?"

These questions mark the beginning of a deeper chapter—the chapter where destiny shifts from something you inherit to something you begin to see clearly.

THE QUIET TURNING POINT WITHIN US

There comes a moment in every person's life when the noise of the world fades just enough for them to hear their own heart again. It doesn't announce itself with drama. It doesn't arrive in a sudden flash of wisdom. It enters quietly, sometimes in the middle of an ordinary day. Maybe you're sitting on a bus, staring out the window. Maybe you're lying awake at night, unable to fall asleep. Maybe you're walking home after a long day, feeling tired in a way you can't explain. Then something shifts inside you. A subtle awareness rises, as if a curtain has been pulled back for just a second, and you sense something true beneath all the layers you've been carrying.

This moment is not loud. It is gentle, almost shy, but once it appears, it never really leaves you.

Understanding your life doesn't begin with answers. It begins with noticing.

You notice the discomfort you once ignored.

You notice the emptiness behind certain routines.

You notice the spark in the rare moments when you feel alive.

You notice the tension between the life you're living and the life quietly waiting inside you.

This noticing is the first step toward understanding destiny. Not destiny as an external force, but destiny as your inner voice—the one that has been trying to speak long before you learned how to listen.

Every person carries two stories inside them. One is the story they were given, shaped by family, environment, culture, and early experiences. The other is the story they wish to live, shaped by their inner nature, desires, values, and quiet truths. Most people spend a large part of their life trying to reconcile these two stories. Some succeed. Some ignore the inner story until it grows faint. Others discover it only when life forces them to stop and look inward.

But the moment you recognize that you have an inner story at all, something powerful begins to change.

There was once a boy named Rayan who grew up believing he needed to meet everyone's expectations. He studied the subjects chosen for him, followed the path laid out before him, and rarely questioned whether any of it matched who he truly was. He wasn't unhappy, but he wasn't fully present either. His life moved forward, but he felt like a silent passenger rather than the person holding the steering wheel.

One day, while helping his younger cousin with a simple art project, he felt something unexpected. As he guided the child's hand across the page, shaping colors and patterns, a feeling of ease washed over him—ease he hadn't experienced in years. It was a small moment, unnoticed by others, yet something inside him lit up. He had forgotten how much he loved creating things. He had forgotten that a piece of him lived in color, not in numbers or expectations.

That brief moment, simple as it was, became the beginning of a shift. Not because he suddenly decided to change everything, but because he finally remembered that there was something within him waiting to be acknowledged. And once remembered, it became impossible to forget.

This is what the quiet turning point looks like. It rarely announces a new path. It simply reminds you that one exists.

Life often brings these reminders through contrast. You realize what you want when you experience what you don't want. You realize who you are when you notice who you pretend to be. You realize what matters when something trivial loses its meaning. You realize what drains you when you find something that energizes you effortlessly.

Understanding destiny is not about predicting the future. It is about understanding these subtle movements within you—the emotions, the memories, the patterns, and the quiet whispers of your deeper self.

Sometimes, clarity arrives through struggle. A relationship breaks down, and you discover parts of yourself you ignored for years. A failure forces you to face the beliefs you carried since childhood. A long period of confusion slowly reveals the truth you were avoiding. These moments may feel heavy, but they are often the spaces where the inner story becomes clear.

There was a woman named Aashi who devoted her entire life to pleasing others. She became the person everyone relied on. She smiled when she was tired, agreed when she wanted to refuse, and took responsibility for things she never caused. She didn't know how to rest, because resting felt selfish. One day, overwhelmed by exhaustion, she sat alone in her room and finally asked herself the question she had been avoiding for years: "What about me?"

The room remained silent, but something inside her responded—not with words, but with a feeling she had forgotten. A feeling of self-worth quietly resurfaced, reminding her that she, too, deserved space. That small moment became her quiet turning point. She didn't change everything at once, but she began the slow process of seeing her own needs as real.

Destiny is not shaped only by the bold decisions people celebrate. It is shaped by soft realizations like these, the ones no one sees, the ones that happen in the privacy of your inner world.

People often think their life changes in big, dramatic ways, but more often, it changes through the small internal shifts that gradually align your outer world with your inner truth. You begin saying yes to things that feel right, and no to things that no longer fit. You begin moving toward people who bring calmness, and away from those who drain your energy. You begin choosing paths that reflect who you are, not who you were taught to be. These changes may seem small, yet each is a quiet turning point, and every turning point reshapes the landscape of your destiny.

The most meaningful understanding comes from recognizing that you are not limited by the story you inherited. You are shaped by it, yes, but not confined to it. The fears you carry, the doubts you hide, the dreams you postpone—all of these were formed in response to earlier moments, earlier environments. And once you understand where they came from, they lose their grip on you.

Life does not demand perfection. It asks for awareness.

Awareness of why you feel the way you do.

Awareness of the patterns you repeat.

Awareness of the dreams you set aside.

Awareness of the moments when your heart speaks louder than your habits.

Understanding destiny is simply understanding yourself in a deeper, more honest way. Not the surface-level version, but the quiet, tender, vulnerable part inside you that has been collecting moments and meanings since the day you were born.

There is something incredibly human about wanting to know where your life is heading. Yet the truth is that destiny is not a distant destination. It is a direction shaped from the inside, step by step, realization by realization. You move toward it whenever you make a choice that feels true, even if that choice is small. You drift away from it when you ignore your inner signals out of fear or habit.

The quiet turning point within you is the beginning of every meaningful change. It appears not when life becomes easier, but when you become more honest with yourself. It appears when you stop running from your inner questions and begin listening to them, even if you don't have answers yet. Answers grow with time. What matters first is noticing.

When you understand this, destiny stops feeling like something written elsewhere. It becomes something you shape gently, patiently, through the way you live your days, the way you interpret your past, the way you respond to the present, and the way you choose your next step. Not a perfect step, just an honest one.

And sometimes, that is enough to begin a new chapter inside you.

TABLE OF CONTENTS

CHAPTER 1: WHY DESTINY AWARENESS CHANGES EVERYTHING

PART 1: THE LIFE WE BUILD WITHOUT REALISING IT

There comes a time in every person's life when they begin to sense that something deeper is at work beneath their everyday routines. You wake up, move through your day, handle responsibilities, face disappointments, celebrate small joys, and fall asleep again. The cycle repeats so often that it begins to feel normal, almost automatic. Yet behind this familiar rhythm, your inner world is quietly shaping the direction of your life.

Most people imagine destiny as something dramatic—something tied to grand opportunities, sudden breakthroughs, or once-in-a-lifetime decisions. But destiny often grows through days that look ordinary. It grows through the way you interpret a setback, the meaning you attach to silence, the thoughts you entertain when no one is watching, and the emotions you carry even when you pretend you don't feel them. A person's direction is not shaped only by what happens to them, but by the inner story they tell themselves about those moments.

Many people move through life without acknowledging this inner story. They believe they are simply reacting to the world around them, unaware that every reaction is influenced by the deeper patterns formed long ago. Without realizing it, a person may carry beliefs that were never truly theirs, fears that came from earlier years, or expectations shaped by others rather than by their own nature. And because these influences work quietly, people assume they are drifting through life without control, when in reality, they are steering themselves in ways they do not yet see.

There is something profoundly human about wanting clarity—wanting to know who you are, where you are heading, and why your life unfolds the way it does. Yet clarity does not arrive through external answers. It arrives through understanding the quiet connection between your inner world and the life you are building, often without noticing.

Imagine a person who always hesitates before taking opportunities. To others, it may look like lack of confidence, but to that person, the hesitation simply feels natural. They may not realize that the hesitation comes from years of being told to stay cautious, or from a moment in childhood when failure felt overwhelming. Without understanding this connection, the person may think life is holding them back, when in truth, it is the inner fear—forgotten but still alive—that is shaping their choices.

Another person may chase achievement endlessly, not because success brings joy, but because praise once filled a gap they didn't know they carried. Someone else may avoid conflict because early experiences taught them that silence keeps peace. Another may feel restless even in comfortable situations, not realizing that their heart is craving growth while their habits keep them in place.

This is why understanding matters.

Not because it gives you control over everything, but because it gives you awareness of yourself.

When people don't understand the forces shaping their choices, they often feel lost. They wonder why some patterns repeat, why certain emotions return, why relationships feel familiar even when the faces are new, or why success sometimes feels strangely empty. This sense of confusion does not come from failure; it comes from living without noticing the quiet influences guiding your direction.

There was a man named Kabir who always felt unsatisfied, no matter how much he accomplished. He changed jobs, moved cities, met new people, and kept telling himself that the next chapter would finally feel right. Yet each time, the same emptiness returned. It wasn't until one evening, when he sat alone with a cup of tea, that something softened inside him. He realized he had spent years chasing accomplishments not because he wanted them, but because he believed they would finally make him feel worthy. That belief didn't come from adulthood; it came from moments in childhood where he was praised only for success and rarely for effort.

That realization didn't transform Kabir instantly. But it helped him understand why his life felt the way it did. And understanding became the beginning of change—not through force, but through awareness.

A person's inner world is powerful. It can lift them, limit them, confuse them, or guide them. When you understand how your thoughts, feelings, memories, and interpretations silently influence your choices, your life begins to make sense in a way it never did before. You stop blaming the world for every pain, and you also stop blaming yourself harshly for every misstep. Instead, you begin seeing the deeper patterns with gentleness, as if finally recognizing a story that has been unfolding inside you all along.

Understanding matters because it frees you from the belief that your path is random.

It replaces confusion with clarity, and heaviness with meaning.

It allows you to see your life as something you are shaping—not perfectly, not completely, but intentionally.

And in that awareness, something shifts.

Life stops feeling like something happening to you.

It begins to feel like something happening through you.

PART 2: THE QUIET IMPACT OF DAILY CHOICES

Most people believe their life changes because of rare moments — moments that feel important, dramatic, or unforgettable. A promotion. A breakup. A new opportunity. A sudden setback. These events certainly shape us, but they are not the true architects of a person's direction. The deeper shaping happens in the moments that go unnoticed, the ones woven into the rhythm of everyday living.

It is the way you speak to yourself when you wake up.

It is the thoughts that fill the silence when you're alone.

It is the emotions you ignore, hoping they will fade.

It is the small decisions you repeat, day after day, until they eventually define your habits.

These moments rarely feel powerful. They feel ordinary, too insignificant to influence anything important. Yet most of what becomes your destiny grows out of these quiet choices. Destiny does not need grand gestures. It grows through the slow, steady accumulation of meanings and patterns you accept without thinking.

There is a young woman named Tara who used to tell herself each morning that she would "try her best today." It sounded positive, almost encouraging, but her tone carried uncertainty. Trying meant she could attempt, then retreat without guilt. For years, she wondered why she always moved half-heartedly, why she gave just enough effort to stay afloat but not enough to move forward. One afternoon, as she reflected on her routine, she finally noticed the tiny phrase she had been repeating daily. "Try" had become her escape. It was a shield from disappointment, a soft excuse she didn't even know she was using. Her destiny wasn't shaped by one big choice — it was shaped by a small sentence she repeated for years.

Another person may begin each day scrolling on their phone for comfort. Ten minutes becomes thirty, and thirty becomes an hour. They never plan for this to influence their future, yet slowly, the daily delay chips away at their energy and direction. They don't lose their dream in a dramatic moment; they lose it quietly through a routine that feels harmless.

This is the hidden truth:

Most people do not drift away from their path through one mistake.

They drift through repeated moments of small neglect.

And most people do not step into their purpose through one breakthrough.

They grow into it through repeated moments of quiet alignment.

Destiny is not a lightning strike. It is a slow sunrise, brightening gradually until you finally recognize the landscape of your life.

Daily choices show who you are becoming long before major events do.

Someone who begins the day with gratitude may slowly become someone who notices beauty even in difficulty. Someone who begins the day with worry may become someone who expects things to go wrong. Someone who keeps choosing comfort may become someone who avoids uncertainty. Someone who takes small steps with intention may become someone who naturally moves with purpose.

These patterns are not dramatic. They are subtle. And because they are subtle, they are powerful.

There was a man named Neil who always waited for the "perfect moment" to begin anything meaningful. He waited for the right mood, the right opportunity, the right environment. Weeks turned into months, and months turned into years. He wasn't lazy. He wasn't uninterested. He simply believed life would open a clear door for him when the time was right.

One morning, while sitting at a café watching people rush by, he realized something strange — almost everyone seemed busy creating their next step, not waiting for it. Some struggled, some stumbled, some smiled through exhaustion, but all of them were moving. And in that moment, Neil felt a quiet understanding settle inside him: the perfect moment was never going to arrive. It wasn't the world that was delaying him. It was his own tendency to wait.

That single realization changed the direction of his life more than any external event ever had.

Understanding destiny matters because it draws your attention to places where you've been living on autopilot. It makes you question routines you once accepted blindly. It helps you see how your smallest choices have been quietly shaping your future. And once you see this, it becomes nearly impossible to live unconsciously again.

Life gains a different texture when you recognize the meaning behind small actions. A conversation becomes more than words; it becomes a window into your emotional patterns. A hesitation becomes more than doubt; it becomes a message from your inner world. A spontaneous idea becomes more than imagination; it becomes a glimpse of your hidden longing.

When you begin to notice the impact of these moments, you understand why destiny matters.

Because destiny is not a force outside you — it is a direction built from within you.

It is created by what you nurture and also by what you neglect.

By what you repeat and also by what you avoid.

By what you believe quietly and also by what you refuse to acknowledge.

Everyday choices may seem small, but nothing small remains small when repeated long enough. Your patterns become your direction, your direction becomes your identity, and your identity becomes the life you eventually call your destiny.

And once you understand this, life stops feeling random.

It begins to feel intentional, even in its uncertainty.

PART 3: WHEN THE HEART SPEAKS BEFORE THE MIND LISTENS

There are moments in life when something inside you speaks long before your thoughts can make sense of it. A strange discomfort. A quiet longing. A sudden stillness in the middle of a familiar routine. These moments often go unnoticed because they rarely come with explanations. They arrive as feelings, not conclusions. And because many people learn to trust logic over emotion, they sometimes dismiss these subtle inner signals.

But if you look back at your life, you'll notice that the most significant turning points weren't always logical. They often began with a feeling — a nudge, a pull, a heaviness, or a spark — that pointed you toward something true.

Some people try to silence these feelings because they fear what they might reveal. Others ignore them because they seem inconvenient. And many simply don't recognize them because they spent years being taught to prioritize external expectations over their inner world. But the heart has its own way of communicating, and it rarely speaks without reason.

Imagine a young woman named Sana. She had a stable job, a predictable routine, and a life that looked perfectly acceptable to everyone around her. Yet every night, when she returned home, she felt an unexplainable heaviness — not sadness, not unhappiness, but something deeper, something quiet. She tried to dismiss it by staying busy, watching shows, or scrolling through her phone, but the feeling always returned. It wasn't loud, but it was persistent.

One weekend, while visiting an art exhibition with friends, she found herself standing in front of a painting that made her feel strangely alive. She couldn't explain why. She simply felt present. It was the first time in years that she felt a shift inside her. And in that moment of stillness, she understood something she had been avoiding: she was living a life that wasn't hers. She had followed a safe path, not a meaningful one. The heart had been speaking long before the mind was ready to listen.

This is why understanding your emotional signals matters.

They are not interruptions.

They are invitations.

Invitations to look closer, feel deeper, and question what you've accepted without examining.

The heart often knows what the mind has not yet processed. It senses when something is out of alignment long before you can put that misalignment into words. It notices the first signs of emptiness, the quiet strain of pretending, and the moments when your true self is being overshadowed by expectations.

Some people confuse these feelings with weakness. They believe emotions make them fragile, when in reality, emotions often make them honest. A person who listens to their inner signals is not unstable; they are aware. They recognize the subtle shifts that many overlook. They sense when something inside needs attention. And they understand that ignoring the heart's whisper eventually turns the whisper into a storm.

There was a man named Vihaan who always felt uneasy during moments that others found exciting. Large celebrations made him feel overwhelmed. Crowded places drained him. Loud environments left him confused. He didn't understand why, so he spent years forcing himself into situations that didn't match his inner nature. He believed something was wrong with him, not realizing that his discomfort was simply a message — a message telling him that his temperament was different, that his soul preferred quiet over noise, depth over surface, meaningful connections over many acquaintances.

The day he understood this, something softened inside him. He stopped judging himself for being different and began allowing himself to exist as he was. His destiny shifted not because the world changed, but because he finally listened to himself.

This is why understanding matters:

It restores your relationship with the truth inside you.

When you understand the difference between fear and intuition, hesitation and misalignment, desire and expectation, everything becomes clearer. You no longer force yourself into places where you don't belong. You no longer apologize for needing what your heart genuinely needs. You no longer chase paths that look good but feel empty. And most importantly, you no longer silence the part of you that notices the truth first.

The heart speaks in moments of rest, moments of overwhelm, moments of joy, moments of discomfort, and moments of longing. It speaks when you meet someone who feels familiar without explanation. It speaks when you walk away from something that doesn't sit right in your soul. It speaks when you encounter a place, a hobby, a dream, or a simple memory that feels strangely sacred to you.

Not every feeling is a direction, but every genuine pull deserves attention.

Life becomes heavy when you live against your inner nature. Choices that look sensible may feel hollow. Achievements that impress others may feel meaningless. Relationships that seem fine may still lack depth. And routines that once felt easy may suddenly feel suffocating. None of this is random. These are signs that something inside you is gently resisting a path that isn't aligned with who you truly are.

Understanding this changes everything.

Not because it solves your problems instantly, but because it gives you a compass.

The compass doesn't tell you exactly where to go, but it tells you where not to stay.

It tells you when something feels wrong, even if you cannot explain why.

It tells you when something feels right, even if you're not ready to embrace it.

It tells you when the story you're living no longer reflects the person you're becoming.

This matters because your destiny is shaped by the direction you lean toward, even before you take the first step. The inner shift always comes before the outer movement. The heart always whispers before the change begins. And the moment you start listening, your life begins unfolding from a place of truth instead of habit.

Understanding what your heart is trying to tell you is not dramatic. It is intimate. It is personal. It is the beginning of clarity — the kind that grows slowly, gently, until one day you realize you are no longer living unconsciously. You are living with awareness of your inner world.

And once you experience that awareness, even once, you never fully return to who you were before.

PART 4: HOW LIFE REVEALS WHAT WE COULD NOT SEE BEFORE

Life has a quiet way of revealing truths at the exact moment you're ready to understand them. Until then, the truth may sit right in front of you, unnoticed, like a book left open on a table that you walk past every day. You don't ignore it intentionally; you simply aren't prepared to read the words yet. Awareness grows the same way. It arrives slowly, often after you've lived through enough experiences to finally connect the dots.

There are moments when the meaning of something becomes clear only after time has passed. A conversation you once dismissed suddenly starts to make sense. An old memory returns, carrying a new significance. A painful experience reveals strength you never knew you had. Clarity does not always come during the moment itself — sometimes it arrives much later, when the heart and mind are finally aligned enough to understand it.

This is why people often say, "I didn't realize it then, but now I see it." Life teaches in hindsight as much as it teaches in real time.

There was a man named Reyansh who spent his early years constantly trying to gain approval. He worked hard, excelled at everything he tried, and made sure everyone around him was satisfied. He thought this meant he was doing well. It wasn't until years later, while looking back at his life, that he realized he hadn't been chasing success — he had been running from rejection. The achievements he celebrated were built on a foundation of fear that he never acknowledged until much later. When he finally understood this, it didn't make his past wrong. It made his present clearer.

Life often becomes meaningful when you begin to understand why you moved the way you did.

Understanding matters because it helps you reinterpret your story with gentleness instead of judgment. It allows you to see that you weren't weak — you were learning. You weren't lost — you were gathering pieces of yourself. You weren't failing — you were evolving in ways you couldn't recognize at the time.

Every experience has a way of shaping you, even when it feels impossible to accept while you're in it.

A heartbreak doesn't just hurt; it shows you the parts of yourself that longed for connection.

A disappointment doesn't just sting; it shows you where your expectations lived.

A moment of joy doesn't just uplift you; it shows you what your soul responds to naturally.

A period of confusion doesn't just unsettle you; it shows you that you're outgrowing your old understanding.

Life is constantly sending signals, but understanding them requires patience.

Some people realize their truth only after years of repeating the same patterns. Others understand it suddenly, triggered by a single moment that shakes their inner world. And some discover it slowly, through small everyday insights that build upon each other until a new picture emerges.

There was a woman named Liana who always felt drawn to quiet places, old libraries, soft music, and gentle conversations. She often forced herself into louder environments because she believed that's what a "normal" young person should enjoy. She never questioned this belief. One day, while helping her friend move into a new house, she found an old journal filled with quotes someone had written long ago. One quote said: *"You do not need to match the world's noise to belong in it."*

The moment she read those words, something inside her relaxed — as if her inner self had finally been acknowledged by the world outside her. She realized she had been trying to change her nature instead of accepting it. This simple moment, triggered by a forgotten notebook, gave her permission to understand herself more honestly.

Life reveals truth when you're ready for it — often through the simplest moments.

Understanding these moments matters because they stitch together the deeper picture of who you are becoming. Without understanding, you may feel like life is a series of random events. With understanding, you begin to see a pattern — a meaningful connection between your experiences, your emotions, your choices, and your growth.

Sometimes, what seemed meaningless becomes the key to something important.

Sometimes, what felt like a setback becomes the reason you developed resilience.

Sometimes, what felt like loss becomes the entry point to a new chapter.

Sometimes, what felt like a mistake becomes the moment that taught you how to see more clearly.

Nothing in your life exists without influencing who you are today.

Understanding doesn't change the past, but it changes the meaning of the past.

And when the meaning changes, the direction of your life changes with it.

Understanding matters because it allows you to reinterpret your story from a place of compassion. You begin to see that the choices you made were the best you could make with the awareness you had at the time. You begin to see that the emotions you carried were responses to moments that shaped you. You begin to see that the patterns you repeated came from a deeper place inside you that was trying to keep you safe.

And once you see your story this way, you no longer feel ashamed of who you were.

You feel curious about who you are becoming.

Every person is continually changing, subtly and silently. Growth is not always visible. Sometimes it appears as a shift in perspective, a softening of anger, a loosening of old attachments, or a newfound ability to sit with your feelings instead of running from them. Growth is not always a leap; sometimes it is a quiet step in the right direction.

That is why understanding matters: it makes you aware of the steps you are taking — even the silent ones.

Life reveals truth slowly, but when you finally see it, everything you once questioned begins to make sense.

PART 5:THE WEIGHT WE CARRY WITHOUT KNOWING

Every person carries a weight that no one else can see. It is not always heavy, not always painful, but it is always present. Some people carry expectations placed on them long before they understood who they were. Others carry untold stories, unspoken fears, forgotten disappointments, or quiet dreams that never found space to grow. This weight shapes the way a person walks through life, even when they believe they have left their past behind.

Often, people assume that the heaviest burdens are the ones that cause visible pain. But the most powerful weights are the silent ones — the beliefs you hold about yourself, the promises you made when you were too young to understand their cost, and the roles you accepted before you realized you had a choice.

There was once a man named Sameer who always felt responsible for keeping peace in his family. He learned early that harmony depended on his ability to stay calm, speak gently, and never express anger. Even as a child, he carried the unspoken rule that he had to hold everything together. As he grew older, this rule stayed buried within him, shaping the way he handled relationships and work. Whenever conflict appeared, he felt the same pressure he felt as a child — the pressure to fix everything.

He never questioned where this weight came from. He simply believed that peace was his duty. It wasn't until years later, during a conversation with a close friend, that he realized he had been carrying a responsibility that was never his alone. Understanding this didn't erase his habit immediately, but it allowed him to place the weight down gently, piece by piece. For the first time in his life, he felt what it meant to breathe without carrying the world on his shoulders.

People carry many kinds of silent weights.

Some carry the fear of failure.

Some carry the fear of not being enough.

Some carry the need to prove themselves.

Some carry the habit of pleasing others.

Some carry guilt from moments they didn't deserve to blame themselves for.

Some carry dreams they buried because they once believed they weren't worthy of them.

These weights do not always shout. They whisper. And because they whisper, they often go unnoticed for years.

A young woman named Haya once said she felt tired even on days when she didn't do much. At first, she thought it was physical exhaustion, but nothing in her lifestyle explained it. Slowly, she began to understand that her exhaustion came from emotional strain — from being overly polite, overly accommodating, overly patient. From holding back her needs to avoid disappointing others. She realized her tiredness wasn't from activity; it was from constantly carrying a role she never questioned.

Understanding the weight you carry is important because the mind becomes lighter the moment it sees what it has been holding all along.

Some burdens are inherited. A child watches their parents struggle, so they grow up believing life is meant to be endured, not enjoyed. Another child grows up in a home where mistakes were punished harshly, so perfection becomes their shield. Someone else grows up surrounded by unpredictability, so control becomes their safety. These patterns continue not because people want them to, but because they learned to survive with them.

Life becomes more compassionate when you understand this. You stop judging yourself for your habits. You stop blaming yourself for your fears. You stop comparing your journey to others who carry different weights.

The weight you carry is shaped by your story.

It is shaped by the silence you kept.

It is shaped by the moments you didn't get to process.

It is shaped by the emotions you hid.

It is shaped by the dreams you postponed.

It is shaped by the love you gave freely, even when you didn't receive it back.

Understanding this matters because it teaches you kindness — the kind you offer to yourself, not just to others.

There was a girl named Leena who grew up being praised for her strength. People admired how she never cried, never complained, and handled everything gracefully. At first, it felt good. She felt proud of being strong. But strength became her armor, and behind that armor, she hid every wound. Years later, she realized she didn't allow herself to feel sadness, not because she didn't have it, but because she didn't feel permitted to express it. She understood then that her "strength" had become a weight. It protected her, but it also isolated her.

When she finally allowed herself to feel what she had been holding back, she discovered a different kind of strength — the strength that comes from honesty, not silence.

This is why understanding your weight matters.

It doesn't remove the challenges of life.

It removes the confusion about why you feel the way you do.

You begin to see your reactions clearly.

You begin to see your patterns without judgment.

You begin to see your emotional habits with compassion.

And slowly, the weight begins to shift.

Some parts of your story will always stay with you, but they don't have to hold you down. When you see them with clarity, they stop being chains. They become chapters — pieces of a larger story you are still writing.

Life feels different when you know what you are carrying. It becomes a little gentler, a little lighter, a little more manageable. You begin to move with awareness rather than habit. You begin to understand the difference between what belongs to you and what you simply picked up along the way.

And as you understand this, something within you begins to settle.

The weight is still there, but it no longer defines your direction.

You are no longer walking blindly under it.

You are walking consciously with it — and eventually, beyond it.

PART 6: THE MOMENTS THAT CHANGE US WITHOUT WARNING

Life does not always give you a sign before it changes you. Some moments arrive softly, almost unnoticed, and yet they shift the way you see everything. You may not recognize their importance at the time. They may feel ordinary, simple, or even inconvenient. But when you look back, you realize that those were the moments that opened something inside you — something you didn't know needed opening.

A change rarely begins with clarity.

It begins with a feeling.

A slight discomfort in a place that once felt familiar.

A quiet longing for something you cannot yet name.

A subtle sense that the life you're living is becoming too small for who you are becoming.

These moments do not shout for attention. They whisper. And because they whisper, many people overlook them. But the people who pay attention discover that their entire direction can shift from a single, gentle realization.

There was a man named Harsh who lived within the safety of routine. He followed the same path to work every day, ate the same meals, and met the same people. Nothing was wrong with his life; it simply felt predictable. One evening, while returning home, he decided to take a different route — not because he planned to, but because he missed his usual turn. That small accident led him through a quiet street lined with old houses and warm lights in the windows. Something about that street made him pause.

He stood there for a few minutes, feeling a peace he hadn't felt in years. In that moment, he realized how long it had been since he slowed down, since he allowed himself to breathe without rushing. He didn't expect the detour to affect him, but it became the moment he understood something deeper: he wasn't tired from work; he was tired from living without presence.

A simple wrong turn became the beginning of a new part of his story.

This is how life changes people — not always through dramatic events, but through quiet shifts that reveal truths hidden beneath daily noise.

Sometimes, the moment that changes you is not a moment of joy or sadness. It can be something as ordinary as the way someone speaks to you with genuine warmth, reminding you of the tenderness you've been missing. It can be a song that touches a memory you didn't realize was still living inside you. It can be a sunrise that makes you pause long enough to realize you haven't looked at the sky in months.

And sometimes, the moment that changes you is the one that breaks your illusion of control.

A plan doesn't work.

A relationship ends.

A dream collapses.

A truth you were avoiding finally surfaces.

These moments feel heavy while they are happening. They stretch your heart, disrupt your rhythm, and force you to sit with emotions you tried to outrun. Yet once the storm settles, something becomes clear — these moments didn't arrive to destroy you; they arrived to reveal something inside you that comfort never could.

There was a young woman named Kiara who spent years planning every detail of her future. She avoided uncertainty because unpredictability frightened her. But life, in its quiet wisdom, does not follow human plans. When she faced a sudden change that she could not control, she was forced to confront a truth she had never admitted: she had been living out of fear, not intention.

The loss she experienced felt overwhelming at first, but as time passed, she began to notice a surprising shift. She felt lighter — not because the pain disappeared, but because she was no longer holding onto the illusion that she had to manage everything perfectly. The moment that once broke her was also the moment that freed her.

Understanding why these moments matter changes the way you see your own journey.

It teaches you that not every difficulty is a punishment.

Not every detour is a mistake.

Not every ending is a failure.

Sometimes, what disrupts your life is guiding you toward a version of yourself that your old life could not accommodate.

Change rarely feels comfortable. It often begins with confusion, resistance, or sadness. But discomfort is not always a sign to retreat. Sometimes, it is a sign that you are stepping into a larger room within yourself — a space you never knew existed because you were too busy surviving the smaller one.

People often say, “Everything happens for a reason,” but the deeper truth is this:

Everything affects you in some way.

Everything reveals something.

Everything teaches you to understand your inner world better.

The meaning doesn’t always appear instantly. Some lessons take time to unfold. Some growth happens quietly, beneath the surface. Some clarity emerges only after you’ve lived enough to interpret the signs.

Life is always in conversation with you, even when you’re not listening.

It speaks through moments of stillness.

It speaks through unexpected changes.

It speaks through the longings you carry but never express.

It speaks through patterns you repeat until you are finally ready to understand them.

When you look back years later, you will see how each moment, even the ones that hurt, played a role in shaping the person you became.

This is why understanding matters.

It helps you see your life not as a series of random experiences, but as a woven story with depth, connection, and meaning.

The moments that change you don't always feel significant when they arrive. But they stay, quietly reorienting your path, guiding you through the unseen spaces within yourself, and reminding you that your story is always unfolding, even when you think nothing is happening.

And when you understand that, you begin to move through life with a gentler heart — one that trusts the inner shifts, respects the quiet signs, and honors the moments that transform you from within.

PART 7: THE DISTANCE BETWEEN WHO WE ARE AND WHO WE APPEAR TO BE

Every person lives with a quiet distance between their inner self and their outer image. This distance is not a mistake; it is part of being human. You present one version of yourself to the world — the version shaped by expectations, responsibilities, and the roles you play. But beneath that outer shell lives the person you truly are, shaped by your feelings, longings, fears, and unspoken truths.

Most people never show their inner self fully. Not because they are dishonest, but because life teaches them to protect certain parts of themselves. Some experiences teach you to hide your vulnerability. Others teach you to keep your dreams quiet. Some teach you to smile even when you're hurting, and others teach you to toughen up because the world doesn't slow down for your pain.

This gap between your outer self and inner self becomes a silent companion. Sometimes, it protects you. Sometimes, it isolates you. But understanding this gap is essential because it explains why people often feel disconnected even in the middle of a busy, successful life.

There was a man named Dev who appeared confident to everyone around him. He spoke with clarity, walked with purpose, and handled challenges with a calm that others admired. Yet inside, he carried doubts that he never shared. These doubts didn't come from weakness. They came from years of being told to "stay strong" and "never show uncertainty." Dev learned to wear confidence like armor, not realizing that his true strength was hidden behind a wall he built long ago.

One day, while talking to a friend who confessed her fears openly, Dev felt something shift inside him. He realized how heavy his armor had become. Her honesty made him aware of the distance he had created within himself. That moment didn't change his life instantly, but it made him more aware of who he appeared to be versus who he actually was. And in that awareness, he felt the first breath of relief he hadn't allowed himself in years.

This distance exists in many forms:

Some people appear cheerful but carry quiet sadness.

Some appear tough but feel fragile inside.

Some appear independent but long for connection.

Some appear social but feel lonely in crowded rooms.

Some appear certain but struggle with doubt every day.

Some appear composed but collapse in private.

None of this is unusual.

None of this is wrong.

This is simply the way human beings learn to move through the world.

But the more this distance grows, the more confused a person feels inside. They begin to lose track of which version of themselves is honest and which is constructed. They may start feeling emotionally tired without knowing why. They may sense that something is missing without knowing what. They may succeed at everything others admire yet still feel disconnected from themselves.

Understanding this distance matters because it helps you see where your emotional energy is going.

Pretending takes effort.

Hiding takes effort.

Adjusting yourself to fit expectations takes effort.

Smiling through discomfort takes effort.

Carrying unspoken stories takes effort.

When you finally understand this, you stop blaming yourself for feeling drained. You realize that emotional exhaustion is not always caused by doing too much — sometimes it is caused by being too far from your true self.

There was a woman named Anika who was known for her warmth and kindness. She comforted everyone, listened to everyone, and always made herself available. To others, she seemed emotionally strong. Yet inside, she felt unseen. She had created a version of herself that made people comfortable, but in doing so, she had hidden the parts of herself that needed comfort too.

One evening, while journaling, she wrote a simple sentence: *"I am tired of being who everyone needs, and forgetting who I am."*

Those words didn't come from sadness. They came from clarity. She realized she had created distance between her inner truth and her outer role. And that distance had slowly drained her over the years.

Understanding this distance does not mean you must reveal your whole self to the world.

It simply means acknowledging that your inner world deserves your attention just as much as your outer responsibilities do.

When you recognize this distance:

You stop holding yourself to impossible standards.

You stop confusing your outer persona with your inner worth.

You stop expecting yourself to be perfect.

You begin treating yourself with the softness you reserve for others.

And slowly, the distance becomes smaller.

It doesn't disappear completely — no one lives without some level of separation between their inner and outer self. But when the gap becomes manageable, life feels more aligned. You no longer feel like you're acting through your days. You feel present in them. You no longer feel like you're living two different lives. You feel integrated — whole.

This is why understanding matters:

Because awareness brings you closer to yourself.

You begin to embrace the parts you once hid.

You begin to accept the feelings you once questioned.

You begin to see beauty in your vulnerability instead of weakness.

You begin to appreciate the courage it takes to live honestly.

And most importantly, you begin to see that the person you show to the world and the person you carry inside you are not enemies. They are companions, learning to walk closer to each other with each step of understanding.

PART 8: WHEN SILENCE TEACHES WHAT WORDS CANNOT

There are times in life when silence becomes more meaningful than anything spoken. Not the silence of emptiness, but the silence that appears when life slows down just enough for you to feel the truth you've been avoiding. This silence does not ask questions. It does not force decisions. It simply creates a space where your inner world can finally breathe without interruption.

Many people fear silence because it exposes the emotions hidden beneath daily noise. In silence, you notice the ache you've been ignoring, the longing you've been suppressing, the tension you've been carrying, and the dreams you've been postponing. Noise distracts the mind. Silence reveals the heart.

There was a young man named Aditya who surrounded himself with constant activity. He filled his days with work, conversations, music, videos, anything that kept him from sitting with himself. On the surface, he looked energetic and social. But deep inside, silence frightened him. It reminded him of the thoughts he didn't want to confront and the emotions he didn't want to feel.

One weekend, during a power outage, he found himself without distractions. No phone, no sound, no activity. For the first time in a long while, he sat in stillness. At first, he felt restless. But slowly, something unexpected happened — he began to understand the heaviness he carried. He realized his constant busyness was not passion; it was escape. Silence didn't punish him. It revealed him.

That quiet moment became the first time he acknowledged himself honestly.

Silence has a way of showing you truths you overlook in noise.

In silence, you notice which thoughts arise naturally and which ones you have been pushing away.

In silence, you realize which feelings are genuine and which ones are habits.

In silence, you sense the parts of your heart that never received your attention.

Understanding this matters because the inner world speaks differently than the outer world.

The outer world uses words.

The inner world uses silence.

Some people experience this silence during long walks. Others during late nights when the world is asleep. Some feel it in nature, some in prayer, some in deep exhaustion, and some in unexpected pauses life creates for them. Regardless of how it arrives, silence invites you to notice what you have been carrying.

There was a woman named Esha who always avoided being alone. She feared that solitude would make her feel lost. But when she moved to a new city for work, she inevitably spent more time with herself. At first, she felt lonely. But after a few weeks, she began to see the beauty in her quiet evenings. She started noticing her own preferences, her own rhythms, her own ideas — things she had never acknowledged because her previous life was filled with constant company.

She didn't become someone else; she became someone she had forgotten.

Silence can be uncomfortable because it doesn't let you hide behind distractions. It removes noise, leaving you with your truth. And facing your truth is not always easy. But the truth, once seen, becomes a bridge — a bridge that connects who you are now to who you are meant to be.

The absence of noise can reveal:

- the relationship you've outgrown,
- the dream you still care about,
- the habit that no longer serves you,
- the pain you still need to acknowledge,
- the peace you've been seeking without realizing it.

And sometimes, silence simply reveals that you are tired — not physically, but emotionally — tired from pretending, from holding back, from carrying roles that are too heavy.

Understanding this matters because silence helps you reconnect with yourself.

It helps you see what your heart has been trying to say beneath the noise of obligation and routine.

It helps you recognize the emotions that remain unresolved.

It helps you notice the small sparks that still make you feel alive.

When you allow silence to speak, you understand things that words cannot explain.

You understand why certain moments hurt more than they should.

You understand why certain people feel familiar even when they're new.

You understand why certain paths feel wrong even when they're right on paper.

You understand the meaning behind your own reactions, your own desires, and your own wounds.

Silence is not empty.

It is full of meaning waiting to be noticed.

And the more you listen, the more you realize that your inner world has always been guiding you — softly, patiently, consistently.

Understanding silence matters because it connects you to the most honest version of yourself.

Not the version shaped by expectations.

Not the version influenced by others 'opinions.

Not the version you show to impress or protect.

Silence connects you to the version that simply is — natural, tender, true.

When you begin to trust that version of yourself, life feels different. You no longer rush through days. You no longer run from your feelings. You no longer fear pauses. Instead, you begin to see them as spaces of clarity — places where insight grows and direction appears without force.

In the quiet moments, you discover that your destiny is not built only through action, but also through awareness.

And awareness grows in silence.

PART 9: WHEN LIFE SLOWS DOWN ENOUGH FOR US TO NOTICE OURSELVES

There are phases in life when everything moves so quickly that you barely recognize the person staring back at you. Days blend into weeks, weeks into months, and somewhere in that blur, your own voice becomes softer. You follow routines because they are familiar. You respond automatically because it is easier. You move through your days almost like a passenger inside your own life.

And then, suddenly, life slows down.

Not always by choice.

Sometimes because a plan falls apart.

Sometimes because your energy fades.

Sometimes because the world becomes quieter.

Sometimes because something inside you refuses to keep going at the same pace.

These slow moments can feel uncomfortable because they pull you out of your usual momentum. But within this discomfort lies the beginning of something essential: **self-recognition**.

There was a woman named Krisha who had spent years chasing speed — more work, more responsibility, more tasks, more accomplishments. She believed movement meant progress. When life finally forced her to slow down due to exhaustion, she panicked. She worried she was falling behind. But as the days passed, she noticed something unexpected. For the first time in years, she could hear herself think without a deadline rushing her thoughts.

She realized she had been living so fast that she forgot what it felt like to live consciously.

The stillness that frightened her in the beginning slowly became a space of clarity.

This is what happens when life slows you down:

You begin to see the parts of yourself you lost in the noise.

You notice the dreams you put aside "for later," without realizing "later" never arrived.

You notice the emotions you never named because you were too busy managing everything else.

You notice how tired you've become from carrying roles that no longer feel like yours.

You notice how much of your life has been shaped by habit rather than intention.

Slowness becomes a mirror — one that reflects the truth you rushed past.

People often misinterpret slow periods as setbacks. They call them dull, unproductive, or wasted. But in reality, these slow periods are essential. They are the places where your heart catches up with your life. They are where your inner world finally gets time to breathe. They are where hidden parts of you rise to the surface, asking to be acknowledged.

There was a boy named Vivaan who struggled with long breaks. He felt restless whenever life gave him too much silence. He believed that if he wasn't constantly doing something, he was failing. But during one long holiday, when he had nothing pressing to complete, he experienced a strange clarity. He began journaling, not out of discipline, but out of curiosity. For the first time, he noticed patterns in his emotions that he had never seen before. He discovered the reasons behind his hesitation, his overthinking, and his sudden bursts of energy.

The break he feared became the moment that introduced him to himself.

Slowness often serves the same purpose.

It pulls back the curtain on your inner world.

In fast moments, you survive.

In slow moments, you understand.

This understanding matters because life is not only about movement; it is about direction.

It is not only about action; it is about awareness.

It is not only about progress; it is about alignment.

When life slows down, you begin to question things you once accepted automatically.

- Why does this routine feel heavy now?
- Why does this relationship feel distant?
- Why does this dream still matter to me after all these years?
- Why am I ignoring a feeling that keeps returning?

These questions don't appear when you're rushing. They appear when you finally pause long enough to hear what your inner world has been trying to say.

Slowness teaches you to look inward — not to fix anything, not to change everything, but simply to recognize yourself again. Because it's possible to live years without noticing who you're becoming. And when you finally recognize yourself, even briefly, something softens inside you. You feel less lost. Less conflicted. Less pressured by the expectations you once blindly carried.

This matters because self-recognition is the foundation of understanding destiny.

You cannot shape a meaningful life if you cannot see yourself clearly within it.

And you cannot see yourself clearly if your life never slows down long enough for reflection.

When life pauses, even for a short moment, it is giving you space — space to feel, to observe, to understand.

Some people use this space to rediscover joy.

Some use it to release burdens.

Some use it to rethink decisions.

Some use it to breathe fully for the first time in years.

And some simply use it to rest, which is itself a form of healing.

Life knows when you need these moments, even when you don't.

It slows you down not to punish you, but to prepare you.

To help you see clearly.

To help you choose consciously.

To help you understand deeply.

Because once you recognize yourself, you begin to move differently — not faster, not louder, but truer.

PART 10: THE BEGINNING OF SEEING YOUR LIFE WITH NEW EYES

There comes a point when understanding becomes more than knowledge. It becomes a shift — a gentle but powerful change in the way you see yourself, the way you interpret your past, and the way you move into your future. This shift is not dramatic. It does not require a loud declaration or a sudden transformation. It begins quietly, almost humbly, with a single realization:

"My life makes more sense when I look at it honestly."

Honesty is not harshness.

It is clarity.

It is the soft light that reveals—not judges.

And when clarity enters, even a little, something inside you settles.

The confusion you once felt begins to loosen.

The heaviness you carried begins to feel lighter.

The mistakes you once replayed in your mind begin to look different.

You stop viewing yourself as someone who failed.

You start seeing yourself as someone who learned.

People often search for big answers—answers that will explain their entire life at once. But understanding rarely arrives in one piece. It arrives in fragments. A moment of awareness here, a small realization there, a quiet connection between two memories, an unexpected insight during a conversation or a silence.

Those fragments eventually form a picture.

Not a perfect picture, but a true one.

There was a man named Ishan who spent years feeling like he wasn't good enough. He couldn't pinpoint why. He simply carried the belief as if it were part of him. One evening, while reflecting on his life, he remembered a moment from childhood—one teacher, one sentence spoken in frustration, one careless remark he took to heart. He didn't realize how deeply that moment shaped him until he saw it again as an adult.

It didn't erase the years of doubt he carried, but it changed the meaning of them. He understood that his belief wasn't born from truth; it was born from a moment he was too young to interpret correctly. Awareness didn't fix everything at once, but it gave him something much more important: **perspective**.

This is why understanding matters.

It doesn't rewrite your story.

It helps you *see* your story.

Understanding creates distance—healthy distance—between you and your old patterns.

You no longer feel controlled by reactions you don't understand.

You no longer feel defined by fears that don't belong to you.

You no longer feel trapped inside beliefs you didn't choose.

Understanding gives you the ability to pause, breathe, and reflect before repeating old habits.

It gives you the space to choose differently—not perfectly, just consciously.

It transforms your journey from unconscious movement into mindful living.

There was a woman named Rhea who described understanding as "taking a deep breath after holding it in for too long." She explained that once she understood why she reacted the way she did, she didn't feel broken anymore. She felt human. She felt like someone who had been shaped by life, not destroyed by it. And that alone changed her direction.

People underestimate how powerful self-understanding is.

It doesn't solve your life, but it softens your struggle.

It doesn't erase your past, but it frees you from misinterpreting it.

It doesn't guarantee certainty, but it offers guidance.

Understanding helps you walk through life with a little more grace.

A little more compassion for yourself.

A little more forgiveness for your story.

A little more trust in your inner compass.

Most importantly, understanding brings you closer to the truth that your destiny is not something outside you waiting to be discovered. It grows from the way you interpret your experiences, the way you connect your past to your present, and the way you choose to move forward with awareness instead of fear.

As this chapter ends, you stand at the beginning of something meaningful — not a conclusion, but a clearer view of yourself. You begin to see why your emotions matter. Why your patterns matter. Why your inner signals matter. Why understanding your story matters.

Because once you see your life with new eyes, you begin to live with new intention.

And once you live with intention, destiny stops feeling like a mystery.

It becomes a direction you can feel from within.

This is where understanding transforms into clarity.

And clarity becomes the first quiet step toward the life waiting ahead of you.

CHAPTER 3: THE INNER VOICE WE OFTEN IGNORE

PART 1: THE MESSAGES HIDDEN IN OUR FIRST REACTIONS

Every person carries a quiet inner voice — not a loud command, not a dramatic message, but a subtle whisper that rises in the very first second of a new experience. This whisper is so gentle that most people overlook it, yet it often holds more truth than the thoughts that follow.

Before your mind analyses, before your fears interfere, before expectations twist your perspective, there is always a first reaction — a natural response that comes from your inner truth. This first reaction is honest. It is unfiltered. It is untouched by pressure or logic or other people's opinions. It simply appears.

Sometimes it appears as a spark of interest.

Sometimes as a sense of discomfort.

Sometimes as a sudden calmness.

Sometimes as a feeling you can't name, but cannot ignore.

This first reaction carries meaning. But because life teaches us to prioritise logic, responsibility, and expectations, many people ignore what they feel in the first second.

There was a girl named Meera who always felt a soft pull toward writing. Whenever she held a pen, something inside her shifted — as if words made her feel alive. But she grew up hearing that writing was not practical, so she brushed off the feeling every time it appeared. She continued down a path that looked sensible but felt hollow. Her first reaction had been trying to guide her, gently, consistently, but she kept placing it aside.

Years later, during a small moment of reflection, she realized that the inner whisper she ignored for so long was never meaningless. It was a glimpse into a part of her that wanted expression long before she knew how to give it space.

This is how the inner voice works — softly, patiently, always present, always ready to guide you, even when you are not ready to listen.

Understanding this matters because the first reaction you feel often reveals:

- what resonates with your inner nature,
- what feels unsafe or misaligned,
- what excites you even before you understand why,
- what drains your energy even when it looks perfect on paper,
- what brings you peace without needing explanation.

Logic comes later.

Fear comes later.

Expectations come later.

But the inner voice comes first.

Someone may walk into a room and instantly feel uneasy, even though everything looks fine.

Another may meet a new person and immediately feel safe, even though they barely know them.

Another may explore a new opportunity and feel a spark of curiosity before they even consider whether it is realistic.

These moments are not accidents.

They are messages — quiet, subtle, and deeply connected to your emotional truth.

There was a man named Aarush who once rejected a job offer for no clear reason. The role was good, the salary was impressive, the company was reputable. Everyone around him insisted he should accept it. But something inside him felt tight whenever he imagined himself there. He couldn't explain it, and because he couldn't explain it, he almost ignored it. Finally, trusting his discomfort, he said no.

Months later, he discovered that the work environment in that company was extremely unhealthy and many employees had resigned. His inner voice sensed something his mind couldn't yet see.

This is why the inner voice matters — it feels the truth before the mind interprets it.

People often ignore this voice because it is quiet, not dramatic. It doesn't demand attention. It simply whispers. And in a world filled with noise, whispers are easy to miss.

But ignoring your first reaction is like walking through life with a dimmed compass. You may still move, still function, still survive — but you lose the clarity of direction that comes from knowing yourself deeply.

When you begin to pay attention to your first reactions, you start noticing patterns:

You feel alive in certain environments.

You feel small in others.

You feel safe with some people immediately.

You feel drained around others without knowing why.

You feel pulled toward certain ideas.

You feel resistance toward paths that don't align with you.

These patterns are not random.

They are clues — hints pointing toward your inner truth.

Understanding your inner voice does not mean you must follow every feeling blindly.

It simply means acknowledging that your emotions hold meaning, even when they don't offer explanations.

Honoring the inner voice is not about impulsiveness.

It is about awareness.

It is the awareness that your first reaction is a form of communication — a quiet message from the deepest part of you, the part untouched by expectations or fear.

Your inner voice does not shout.

It doesn't need to.

It reveals itself in the smallest moments, trusting that one day you will learn to listen.

And when you do, life begins to feel less confusing and more aligned.

Not perfect, not predictable — simply clearer.

Because you are no longer navigating blindly.

You are listening to the guidance that has always been with you, waiting patiently beneath the noise.

PART 2: THE TRUTH THAT RISES WHEN WE STOP PRETENDING

Most people move through life carrying versions of themselves they created to fit in, to survive, or simply to avoid conflict. These versions are not lies — they are protections. Masks shaped slowly over time, sometimes so naturally that the person wearing them forgets they exist.

You become polite when you want to scream.

You become strong when you want to rest.

You become agreeable when you want to speak.

You become cheerful when you feel empty.

You become independent when you are craving closeness.

These masks aren't mistakes.

They are responses — shaped by experiences, formed by expectations, reinforced by fear.

But beneath every mask lives a quieter truth.

A truth that emerges only in private moments, when you're not performing for the world, when you're not trying to match someone's expectations, when you're not carrying roles that drain you.

This truth is gentle, but persistent.

It returns when the noise disappears.

It whispers through your emotions, your silences, your longings, and your discomforts.

It reminds you that who you pretend to be is not always who you truly are.

There was a girl named Aira who spent years laughing at jokes she didn't find funny, agreeing with opinions she didn't believe in, and joining groups she didn't feel connected to. She wasn't trying to deceive anyone. She simply didn't want to stand out or create tension.

One evening, while sitting alone in her room after a long social gathering, she felt an unexpected sadness — not because anything bad had happened, but because she couldn't remember the last time she was genuinely herself. The mask she wore had become so automatic that she forgot what her own voice sounded like.

That moment didn't fix everything.

But it revealed something important:

Her sadness wasn't coming from loneliness — it was coming from self-abandonment.

This is what the inner voice reveals when you stop pretending.

It shows you the parts of yourself you've silenced.

The dream you buried because it didn't fit others 'expectations.

The boundaries you ignored because you didn't want to upset anyone.

The emotions you held in because expressing them felt unsafe.

The opinions you softened because you feared being judged.

The exhaustion you hid because the world praised your strength.

When you stop pretending, even briefly, the truth rises to the surface — fragile, honest, and often surprising.

Some people fear this truth because it challenges the identities they've built.

Others avoid it because they don't want to disappoint the world around them.

And many simply don't know how to express the person they've kept hidden for so long.

But the inner voice does not disappear.

It waits.

It watches.

It whispers through the cracks in your mask.

There was a man named Zayd who always acted confident. He stood tall, spoke loudly, and laughed freely. People described him as bold, fearless, and charismatic. Yet every night, he felt a quiet emptiness — as if the person the world admired wasn't the person he actually was. For years, he ignored the discomfort. But during a long conversation with an old friend, he found himself admitting, "Sometimes I feel like I'm performing my own life."

That small confession became his turning point.

Not because it solved everything — but because it was the first time he allowed his inner truth to breathe.

Understanding this matters because the inner voice is often suppressed by the versions of ourselves we show to others.

The more you pretend, the quieter your truth becomes.

The quieter your truth becomes, the more disconnected you feel.

Pretending drains you in a way physical labor never could.

It is tiring not because you're weak, but because the soul grows heavy when it is not allowed to be seen.

But when you stop pretending — even for a moment — something inside you softens. Something that has been tense for years relaxes quietly, like a tight knot beginning to loosen.

You feel a flicker of relief.

A breath you didn't know you were holding finally releases.

A part of you whispers, "This is me."

Understanding that moment is important.

Because the inner voice you ignore today becomes the ache you feel tomorrow.

And the ache you ignore tomorrow becomes the emptiness you feel years later.

Listening to your inner voice is not rebellion.

It is reunion — a reunion with the self you abandoned in the process of pleasing the world.

You do not need to remove your masks all at once.

You simply need to recognize that they exist.

Because once you see them, you can choose when to wear them and when to let them go.

And in that choice, you return to the truth inside you — the truth that has been waiting patiently beneath every layer of silence.

PART 3: THE CONFUSION WE FEEL WHEN WE GO AGAINST OURSELVES

There is a unique kind of confusion that appears when your actions do not match your inner truth. It's not the confusion that comes from lack of information or uncertainty about the world — it's the confusion that comes from acting in ways that contradict what you quietly know inside.

This confusion is subtle.

It appears as restlessness.

As irritability.

As unexplained sadness.

As sudden tiredness after simple tasks.

As a feeling that something is "off," even when you cannot articulate why.

Many people misinterpret this confusion as mood swings or stress. But more often than not, it is your inner voice signaling that you're living against yourself — that your choices are moving in a direction your heart does not want to follow.

There was a man named Rohan who accepted a job everyone told him was "perfect." On the outside, it truly looked ideal — good pay, stability, respect. But every morning, he woke up with a heaviness that he didn't understand. He wasn't facing any particular problem, yet something inside him resisted the path he was walking.

For months, he tried to silence that feeling. He told himself he was ungrateful, weak, or just adjusting. But the confusion persisted until one evening, while staring at his computer screen, he realized something simple but profound: *his outer life made sense to the world, but not to him.*

That realization did not give him immediate answers, but it gave him clarity — the clarity to understand that his confusion wasn't random. It was a message.

This kind of emotional confusion appears whenever you force yourself into a life that doesn't match who you are becoming.

Some people feel it in relationships where they shrink to fit someone else's comfort.

Some feel it in career paths that look impressive but feel lifeless.

Some feel it in routines that keep them safe but not fulfilled.

Some feel it in choices they make to please others rather than honor themselves.

Confusion is often not a sign of being lost.

It is a sign of self-betrayal.

When you move against your inner truth, your mind tries to adapt — but your heart resists.

When you choose silence over honesty, your emotions grow louder inside.

When you ignore your needs, your body feels heavier.

When you pretend to be fine, your inner voice whispers through discomfort.

This inner resistance is not sabotage; it is protection.

It is your deeper self trying to guide you back toward alignment.

There was a girl named Sara who always said yes to everything. She didn't want to disappoint anyone. She agreed to plans even when she was exhausted. She helped others even when she had nothing left to give. She smiled through moments that made her uncomfortable. Over time, she started feeling confused — not about the world, but about herself. Her yeses didn't feel like yeses. Her boundaries didn't feel like boundaries. She couldn't understand who she was anymore.

One day, while declining a plan for the first time in months, she felt strange relief — a relief so strong it startled her. That single "no" brought clarity she had been missing.

She realized the confusion she carried came from living a life built on avoiding disappointment rather than honoring her truth.

This is why understanding your inner voice matters — not because it solves all problems, but because it helps you identify when the disconnection you feel is actually a signal.

A signal telling you:

- You are drifting away from your true self.
- You are repeating patterns that don't belong to you anymore.
- You are living through expectations that suffocate your spirit.
- You are ignoring emotions that want attention.
- You are choosing paths you've outgrown.

Confusion is a form of clarity when you learn to interpret it.

It doesn't tell you what to do — it tells you something is wrong.

And that awareness is powerful.

Many people force themselves to endure situations that slowly empty them because they don't understand the meaning of their confusion. They mistake their emotional resistance for weakness instead of recognizing it as inner guidance.

But the truth is simple:

When your actions move away from your inner truth, your emotions create friction.

This friction appears as confusion.

And confusion is the heart's way of saying, "Please pay attention."

Understanding this changes the way you experience your life.

You no longer blame yourself for feeling lost.

You no longer judge yourself for feeling unsure.

You begin to see the wisdom behind your emotions, not the chaos.

Because your inner world always knows the truth — the truth you are trying to grow toward, the truth you are trying to protect, the truth you are trying to remember.

Listening to that truth is not easy. It requires honesty. It requires patience. It requires the courage to question the life you've built. But the moment you acknowledge it, even gently, the confusion begins to settle.

Not because everything is fixed, but because you finally stopped going against yourself.

PART 4: THE PULL TOWARD WHAT FEELS LIKE HOME

Every person has a certain kind of environment, energy, or experience that feels like "home" to them — not a physical home, but an emotional one. It's the feeling of belonging, of ease, of being understood without explanation. This sense of home doesn't always match where you grew up or who you grew up with. It often reveals itself later in life, in unexpected moments, in surprising places, or through people you never imagined would feel familiar.

This feeling is the inner voice trying to guide you.

Some feel at home in quiet places, some in lively spaces.

Some feel at home with deep conversations, some in simple laughter.

Some feel at home with creativity, some with meaningful routines.

Some feel at home with people who challenge them, some with people who ground them.

The heart recognizes home faster than the mind does.

There was a woman named Noor who moved to a new city for work. It was loud, crowded, busy — everything she thought she wanted. Yet every evening she returned home feeling a strange emptiness. One weekend, she visited a small, calm café tucked away from the main streets. The moment she stepped inside, she felt her entire body relax. She didn't understand why, but something about that quiet corner felt like home.

She sat there for hours, writing in her notebook, sipping tea, absorbing the stillness. It was in that moment she realized she had been chasing the idea of an exciting life, not the life that actually nourished her. Her inner voice had known it all along; she just hadn't slowed down enough to listen.

This is how the inner voice works — it pulls you toward what feels like home long before you understand the reason.

Sometimes, home is not a place.

It's a moment.

A feeling.

A certain kind of person.

A version of yourself.

There was a boy named Zehan who always felt restless among large groups. But the moment he found someone he could share honest thoughts with, he felt a peace he didn't know he was missing. He understood then that "home" for him wasn't about popularity or full rooms — it was about depth, sincerity, and emotional safety.

Your inner voice always pulls you toward what feels emotionally true, even if you don't realize it.

You may feel drawn to certain hobbies without knowing why.

You may feel a soft pull toward certain people because your soul feels understood.

You may feel at peace in nature even if you never grew up around it.

You may feel alive while listening to music, painting, writing, or exploring ideas that others don't understand.

These pulls are not random.

They are signals — gentle reminders of who you are beneath the layers of expectation.

The places where you feel most like yourself are the places where your inner voice speaks the loudest.

Many people ignore these pulls because they don't match the life they think they "should" want. They chase achievements, status, or familiar patterns while quietly longing for something that feels more authentic. The world often teaches you to choose what looks good rather than what feels like home.

But your inner voice knows the difference.

It knows when a path feels natural.

It knows when a person feels safe.

It knows when a routine drains you.

It knows when a dream still lives inside you.

Even before you admit it, your inner world already knows where your heart belongs.

There was a man named Yuvraj who grew up in a practical family. Dreams were considered distractions, and emotions were rarely discussed. He followed a stable path, but whenever he played the guitar, something in him woke up. He felt alive, expressive, seen — even if no one was watching. That feeling was home. He didn't need applause or validation. The feeling itself was enough to tell him that a piece of his destiny lived in that sound.

Understanding this pull matters because it reveals the truth you cannot see with logic alone.

Your inner voice guides you through feeling, not instruction.

Through comfort, not reasoning.

Through resonance, not explanation.

When something feels like home, it is your heart recognizing a piece of itself.

People often ask, "How do I know what I truly want?"

The answer is simple: **Notice what feels natural. Notice what brings peace. Notice what wakes something inside you. Notice what feels like home.**

This recognition does not require you to change your life immediately.

It simply asks you to honor the truth of what your heart knows.

Because the places, people, and moments that feel like home are not coincidences — they are reminders.

Reminders of your inner nature.

Reminders of your emotional needs.

Reminders of the life that aligns with who you are.

And when you pay attention to these reminders, the path ahead becomes clearer — not perfect, not predictable, but undeniably true.

PART 5: THE QUESTIONS WE AVOID BECAUSE THEY REVEAL TOO MUCH

Every person carries questions inside them — quiet questions that rise in moments of stillness but are often pushed away because their answers feel too heavy, too honest, or too revealing. These questions are not loud. They appear like small thoughts, short pauses, or subtle discomforts that sit at the edges of your mind.

Questions such as:

"Is this really the life I want?"

"Why do I feel distant from myself?"

"What am I running from?"

"Why does this not feel like enough?"

"Why do I feel lost even when everything looks fine?"

These questions seem simple, but beneath them lies truth — truth that has been waiting to be acknowledged.

People avoid these questions not because they don't care, but because they sense that the answers may require them to confront parts of their life they aren't ready to face. Change often begins with a question, and change is frightening. So many choose silence instead.

But avoiding a question doesn't make it disappear.

It simply turns into a quiet weight that follows you.

There was a man named Rehan who spent years convincing himself he was satisfied. He had stability, comfort, and predictability — things many people desire. But at night, when the world grew quiet, he felt a strange emptiness. He often brushed it off, telling himself, *"I'm just tired. It's nothing."*

But the question kept returning:

"Is this really my path?"

Rehan avoided it because it threatened the life he had built. But one evening, while watching someone speak passionately about their work, he felt a sudden ache in his chest — not jealousy, but recognition.

Recognition that he wanted to feel alive too.

Recognition that he had been avoiding the truth his inner voice had known for years.

The question he avoided the most was the one that finally revealed who he was.

This is how inner questions work:

They rise again and again until you cannot ignore them anymore.

Some question relationships.

Some question routines.

Some question careers.

Some question identity.

Some question dreams left behind.

Some question the roles they accepted without thinking.

These questions are not meant to break your life apart.

They are meant to help you understand your life more authentically.

Avoiding them only postpones clarity.

Facing them opens a door you didn't know you needed.

There was a woman named Shyla who once said she felt like she was "living but not alive." When she finally allowed herself to sit with that statement, she realized she had been avoiding emotions she didn't want to feel — disappointment, grief, longing, and even hope. Each avoided emotion turned into an unasked question:

“What part of me have I silenced?”

“What dream have I abandoned?”

“What truth am I afraid to say out loud?”

Her healing didn’t begin with answers.

It began with the courage to ask the questions.

This is why the inner voice is so important.

It doesn’t push you toward action immediately.

It simply invites you to be honest with yourself.

Honesty is the foundation of any real transformation.

And honesty always begins with a question.

People fear inner questions because they assume the answers will demand drastic changes — ending relationships, leaving jobs, breaking routines. But most of the time, the answers do something far gentler:

They help you understand yourself.

They help you stop pretending.

They help you stop blaming yourself for feelings you couldn’t explain.

They help you be kinder to the parts of you that you once judged.

Understanding the questions is sometimes enough to shift your entire direction.

There was a boy named Arnav whose life looked perfect on the outside. He excelled at everything, had friends, and met everyone’s expectations. But inside, he carried one persistent question:

“Why do I feel like something is missing?”

For years, he ignored it because he felt guilty. He believed he should be grateful. But gratitude and longing can exist together. Gratitude honors what you have. Longing points to what you need.

The day Arnav stopped avoiding his question was the day he realized he wanted a life that allowed him to feel, not just perform.

That single realization changed his relationship with himself.

This is why inner questions matter:

They reveal what your heart knows but your mind hasn’t accepted yet.

You don’t have to answer everything right away.

You don’t have to change your life overnight.

You don’t have to fear the truth inside you.

You simply need to listen.

Because the questions you avoid often become the keys that unlock the deeper parts of your destiny — the parts waiting patiently behind the life you’ve been living so far.

PART 6: THE FEELINGS THAT RETURN AGAIN AND AGAIN FOR A REASON

Every person has certain feelings that keep returning, no matter how much they try to suppress them. These feelings are not random. They follow you through different phases of life, appearing in new situations, resurfacing in quiet moments, whispering the same message in different ways.

Some feelings return because they carry unresolved truth.

Some return because they are reminders of who you are.

Some return because they reveal what you deeply need.

Some return because they highlight what you have outgrown.

No matter the reason, returning feelings are signals — gentle, persistent signals.

There was a woman named Diya who always felt a deep restlessness whenever she stayed in the same routine for too long. She tried to silence it by keeping herself busy, by convincing herself she should be "grateful," by pushing her feelings aside. But the restlessness always returned. Even in new places, even with new people, even with new achievements.

One night, while walking alone, she realized that the restlessness wasn't a sign of dissatisfaction with her life — it was a sign that she was meant for more growth, more exploration, more emotional expansion than she allowed herself. The feeling she tried to silence was actually guiding her.

This is how returning feelings work.

They persist until you acknowledge them.

Some people keep feeling drained in certain environments.

Some feel anxious in situations where they must pretend.

Some feel heavy around people who do not value them.

Some feel alive when doing something creative, even if they call it "just a hobby."

Some feel a pull toward a dream they abandoned.

Some feel a quiet sadness that signals something missing.

These feelings return because they hold information your mind has not yet processed.

When a feeling repeats itself, it's not a flaw.

It's a message.

There was a man named Viraj who always felt uneasy after conversations where he agreed too quickly. The discomfort wasn't loud, but it lingered. He thought he was overly sensitive, but over time he realized something deeper: the discomfort appeared whenever he betrayed his true thoughts. His inner voice wasn't criticizing him — it was nudging him toward authenticity.

Returning feelings are often your inner compass trying to guide you back to yourself.

People often dismiss these feelings because they seem inconvenient.

They fear what they might reveal.

They think the feelings are "silly," "dramatic," or "unnecessary."

But feelings don't return without purpose.

A longing that keeps resurfacing is telling you where your heart still lives.

A sadness that keeps visiting is showing you what needs healing.

A desire that won't disappear is pointing toward your deeper truth.

A dream you can't forget is reminding you of who you were before fear took over.

There was a girl named Imani who felt drawn to painting since childhood. But she ignored the feeling for years because life became practical, busy, demanding. Yet every time she touched a brush —

even by accident, even casually — she felt a spark she couldn't deny. That spark was her inner voice trying to remind her of a forgotten piece of herself.

Returning feelings remind you of what truly matters.

Ignoring them doesn't make them disappear.

It only delays your understanding.

Some people feel the same fear repeatedly not because they're weak, but because there is something inside that needs attention.

Some feel the same excitement again and again because their soul is pointing toward a path they're meant to explore.

Some feel the same discomfort because they're living against their nature.

Your emotions repeat themselves for a reason.

The mind forgets.

The heart remembers.

And the body responds.

This is why understanding your inner voice matters — because returning feelings reveal truths that the mind tries to hide, soften, or explain away.

When you begin to pay attention to these patterns, you gain clarity:

You realize which people uplift you and which drain you.

You notice which situations make you shrink and which make you grow.

You see which parts of your life feel forced and which feel effortless.

You understand which dreams are temporary impulses and which are permanent desires.

You recognize which emotions belong to the past and which belong to your present.

Understanding these feelings does not force you to act immediately.

It simply helps you see the truth.

And once you see the truth, you cannot unsee it.

Returning feelings are not interruptions.

They are guidance.

They come back because they want to be heard.

And they are part of the map you carry inside — the map that leads you toward your most authentic life.

PART 7: THE PEACE THAT APPEARS WHEN YOU STOP FIGHTING YOURSELF

There is a certain kind of peace that arrives not when life becomes easier, but when you stop going against your own inner truth. This peace is not dramatic or loud. It doesn't come with celebration or applause. It comes quietly, almost secretly, in the moments when you finally let yourself be who you really are.

Most people spend years fighting themselves without realizing it.

They fight their feelings.

They fight their needs.

They fight their longings.

They fight their natural temperament.

They fight the voice inside that keeps trying to tell them the truth.

This internal struggle is exhausting.

Not because life is hard, but because pretending is.

Not because you're weak, but because resisting your inner truth requires constant effort.

There was a woman named Kavya who always portrayed herself as confident and carefree. She acted strong even on days she felt fragile. She said "I'm fine" even when her heart felt heavy. She tried to be someone who never needed help.

But deep inside, she longed for gentleness — for deeper conversations, for emotional closeness, for understanding.

The day she allowed herself to admit this, she didn't change her entire life. She simply stopped fighting the softness she had hidden for so long. That single act brought her more peace than years of pretending ever did.

Peace doesn't come from forcing yourself into a version of life that doesn't match your nature.

It comes from aligning your inner world with your outer choices.

There was a man named Shaurya who spent his youth trying to impress others. He changed his behavior based on who he was with. He laughed louder, acted bolder, spoke differently depending on the crowd. It wasn't dishonesty — it was survival. But the more he adapted outwardly, the more he lost connection with his inner self.

One evening, after leaving a gathering where he felt exhausted, he sat alone in his room and whispered a sentence he had never admitted out loud:

"I'm tired of performing myself."

In that moment, something inside him settled. He realized he didn't need to earn his place by being someone else. The peace he felt wasn't from solving anything — it was from finally being honest with himself.

This is what inner peace truly is:

Not the absence of problems,

but the absence of inner conflict.

When you stop fighting yourself, life becomes lighter even when nothing around you changes.

Your days feel softer.

Your choices feel clearer.

Your emotions feel easier to understand.

Your relationships feel more natural.

Because you're no longer carrying the heavy weight of pretending.

Many people believe peace comes from controlling everything around them.

But real peace comes from releasing the pressure inside you —

the pressure to please,

the pressure to fit in,

the pressure to achieve constantly,

the pressure to hide your true emotions,

the pressure to meet expectations you never chose for yourself.

When these pressures soften, your inner truth has room to breathe.

There was a girl named Manvi who always called herself "too sensitive." She tried to toughen up because she believed sensitivity was a weakness. She forced herself into routines that drained her, conversations that overwhelmed her, and environments that felt too loud for her spirit.

But the more she fought her sensitivity, the more anxious she became.

One day, while watching a quiet sunset, she felt something shift. She realized her sensitivity wasn't the enemy — it was her guide. It helped her understand people deeply. It made her compassionate. It allowed her to feel beauty intensely. For the first time, she stopped fighting her nature.

That acceptance brought her a peace she had been searching for everywhere else.

Peace appears the moment you stop trying to rewrite who you are.

The inner voice becomes louder when you stop resisting the parts of yourself that you once judged.

It guides you with clarity.

It nudges you gently.

It points you toward choices that feel natural.

Understanding this matters because so much of human suffering comes not from circumstances, but from the internal war people wage with themselves.

When you stop this war —

when you accept your emotions,

honor your needs,

respect your temperament,

and acknowledge your desires —

you stop breaking your own heart.

And the moment you stop breaking your own heart, peace begins to grow.

Not perfect peace.

Not constant peace.

But a steady, quiet peace — the kind that stays even in the middle of life's noise.

Because it comes from alignment, not escape.

From truth, not pretending.

From acceptance, not resistance.

And once you experience this inner peace, even briefly, you begin to understand why listening to your inner voice matters more than anything else —

because it leads you back to yourself.

PART 8: THE GENTLE WARNINGS WE OVERLOOK UNTIL THEY HURT

Life rarely sends loud warnings when something isn't right for us.

Instead, it begins with subtle signs:

A slight discomfort in a place that once felt familiar.

A hesitation when your mind tells you to be excited.

A heaviness in conversations you used to enjoy.

A quiet dread about routines you once found normal.

A small voice whispering, *"This isn't you anymore."*

These are the gentle warnings — the early signals from the inner voice.

But because these signals are soft, most people dismiss them.

They push forward, telling themselves:

"It's just a phase."

"I'm overreacting."

"I should be grateful."

"Everyone feels this way sometimes."

"It'll go away."

And sometimes, it does go away — for a moment.

But when the same feeling returns again and again, stronger each time, it is no longer a passing emotion.

It is a message.

There was a man named Om who stayed in a job that drained him emotionally. At first, he felt small hints of discomfort — minor irritations, slight frustration, a lack of motivation. He ignored these warnings because they didn't seem serious. But as weeks turned into months, the discomfort grew heavier. His energy faded. His creativity dulled. His mornings felt heavier than his nights.

By the time he finally acknowledged how deeply the job was affecting him, the gentle warnings had already become loud.

His inner voice had been trying to protect him long before he realized he needed protection.

This is what happens when we ignore the early signals —

they grow louder until we can no longer outrun them.

Life whispers before it shouts.

The heart nudges before it breaks.

The soul warns before it collapses.

There was a woman named Jiya who stayed in a friendship that slowly turned one-sided. She kept giving and giving, hoping things would return to how they once were. But small signs kept appearing — her tiredness after each conversation, her anxiety before meeting that friend, her disappointment when kindness was never reciprocated.

She ignored these signs because she didn't want to lose the relationship.

But the warnings grew stronger until one day she reached emotional exhaustion.

Her inner voice had been whispering the truth long before she reached that point.

Gentle warnings appear in all areas of life:

- The job that drains you
- The person who pulls you down
- The dream that no longer fits
- The routine that feels suffocating
- The habits that keep you stuck
- The boundaries you've been avoiding
- The conversations that leave you empty

These moments may seem small, but they hold deep significance.

Your inner voice always tries to protect your emotional well-being.

It shows you discomfort not to punish you, but to guide you.

It sends warnings not to scare you, but to help you see clearly.

But clarity requires listening.

There was a boy named Aayush who felt uneasy every time he compromised his values to impress others. Each time he did so, he felt a tightness in his chest — a small, physical signal that something wasn't right. But he kept ignoring it because he feared judgment.

It took him years to understand that the discomfort was never about fear — it was about self-betrayal.

His inner voice was trying to save him from losing himself.

Gentle warnings are the emotional footprints of your inner truth.

They show you where not to walk.

They show you which situations are draining your spirit.

They show you which environments no longer match your growth.

They show you the places where your heart feels unsafe or unseen.

And the sooner you understand these warnings, the easier your life becomes.

Ignoring them only delays the truth.

Listening to them brings clarity long before pain arrives.

The inner voice does not want you to suffer to learn a lesson.

It tries to guide you softly, gradually, patiently.

But when the soft guidance is ignored, life eventually becomes louder — not out of cruelty, but out of necessity.

You may feel guilt for wanting to walk away from something that no longer feels right.

You may feel confusion about why something once comfortable now feels foreign.

You may feel fear about acknowledging the signals you've been avoiding.

But gentle warnings are not judgments.

They are insights.

They are early signs of misalignment.

They are invitations to protect your peace before your peace collapses.

When you begin listening to these early signals, you begin living with awareness.

You begin making choices that honor your emotional truth rather than deny it.

You begin avoiding situations that drain you before they overwhelm you.

You begin walking away from noise before it becomes chaos.

You begin choosing paths that feel right instead of simply looking right.

And in that awareness, you discover something beautiful:

Life becomes softer when you listen early.

And your heart becomes lighter when you stop ignoring what it has been trying to tell you all along.

PART 9: THE VERSIONS OF OURSELVES WE GROW OUT OF

Every person carries older versions of themselves inside — versions shaped by past experiences, old fears, beliefs inherited from childhood, and habits learned through survival. These versions once served a purpose. They helped you navigate situations you didn't understand yet. They protected you when you didn't have the strength or awareness to protect yourself.

But there comes a time when certain versions of you no longer fit the life you are trying to create.

You may still carry the cautious child who learned to stay quiet to avoid conflict, even though you are now surrounded by people who would listen if you spoke.

You may still hold on to the perfectionist teenager who believed mistakes made you unworthy, even though you now understand that growth requires imperfection.

You may still follow the habits of a person you no longer are — habits created in different chapters, for different circumstances, for a different version of you.

And because these old versions live inside you, they sometimes shape your choices without your awareness.

There was a woman named Sana who grew up believing she needed to achieve constantly to earn love. This belief shaped her entire identity. She pushed herself relentlessly, always chasing the next milestone, never allowing herself to rest. As an adult, her life looked impressive from the outside, but inside, she felt hollow.

One evening, during a quiet moment, she realized she was no longer the child who needed to prove her worth. Yet she was still living as if she was.

Her old version was making decisions her present self no longer agreed with.

This is what happens when you carry earlier versions of yourself into your present life —

your inner world becomes crowded with outdated beliefs.

It isn't your fault.

It is simply a sign that you are growing.

There was a man named Neil who spent his early years being overly cautious because his environment was unpredictable. Caution became his survival tool. But as an adult, that caution turned into hesitation. Even when opportunities were safe, he held himself back. One day, he realized he wasn't protecting himself anymore — he was limiting himself.

The version of him that once needed caution was now preventing him from living.

You cannot blame your past self for how they behaved.

They did what they had to do.

But you also cannot let those old versions decide your future.

Growth often feels uncomfortable because it requires letting go of pieces of yourself that once felt like home.

Not because they were wrong, but because they have completed their purpose.

There was a girl named Naina who had always been the "peacekeeper" in her family. She learned to avoid conflict, to stay agreeable, to keep everyone comfortable. But as she entered adulthood, she felt a growing frustration — not at others, but at herself. She realized she had outgrown the version of herself who kept silent to maintain harmony. Her inner voice was urging her to speak, to express, to exist fully.

Letting go of her old version didn't mean disrespecting her past.

It meant honoring her present.

This is the gentle truth:

You are allowed to outgrow the person you once needed to be.

You are allowed to release the defenses that no longer serve you.

You are allowed to let go of beliefs built from outdated pain.

You are allowed to stop replaying old fears.

You are allowed to evolve beyond what your past environment taught you.

You are allowed to create a new identity based on awareness, not survival.

Outgrowing old versions of yourself doesn't happen all at once.

It happens slowly, through quiet realizations, emotional shifts, repeated patterns, and small moments of self-awareness.

Sometimes, you grow out of a dream you once chased passionately.

Sometimes, you grow out of a friendship that once felt like family.

Sometimes, you grow out of habits that once protected you.

Sometimes, you grow out of expectations that were never truly yours.

This growth is not betrayal.

It is evolution.

There was a boy named Aarav who once believed he wasn't capable of achieving much. This belief came from years of being compared, judged, and underestimated. But as he grew older, he began noticing moments where he proved that belief wrong. Small successes, new strengths, unexpected confidence. Slowly, the old version of himself — the one who felt small — began to fade. Not because he rejected that version, but because he no longer lived inside it.

You are allowed to thank your previous versions for helping you survive.

You are allowed to appreciate the lessons they taught you.

But you are also allowed to step forward without carrying them the entire way.

Understanding which version of you is speaking helps you understand why you feel what you feel.

Is it the current you who is scared?

Or a younger version who hasn't healed?

Is it the present you who is hesitant?

Or a past version who was once hurt?

Is it the real you who doubts your worth?

Or an old belief still lingering inside?

When you begin to understand this, your inner world becomes clearer.

You stop blaming yourself for old reactions.

You stop judging yourself for old fears.

You begin to see that certain emotions aren't flaws — they are remnants of who you used to be.

And the moment you recognize this, something inside you softens.

You stop fighting yourself.

You stop feeling broken.

You stop carrying outdated identities.

You begin stepping into who you are now.

Not who you were.

Not who you pretended to be.

Not who others expected you to be.

But the person your inner voice is guiding you toward —

the version of you that feels true.

PART 10: RETURNING TO YOURSELF, ONE HONEST MOMENT AT A TIME

There comes a point in every person's life when the path ahead stops being shaped by external expectations and begins to be guided by a quieter truth rising from within. This shift doesn't happen in an instant. It happens slowly, through a collection of honest moments — moments where you meet yourself without the masks, without the noise, without the pressure to be anything other than what you truly are.

The journey of listening to your inner voice is not about perfection.

It is about gentleness.

It is about understanding.

It is about returning to yourself, piece by piece.

Many people believe that finding clarity requires dramatic change — leaving everything behind, shifting their entire life, or reinventing themselves completely. But clarity rarely demands such extremes.

It grows in small choices.

It appears in quiet realizations.

It forms when you stop running from truths that have been waiting inside you.

There was a woman named Mira who spent years ignoring her inner discomfort. She told herself she was fine, that everything was manageable, that her needs could wait. But one morning, while sitting alone before work, she felt an unexpected calm while simply acknowledging how tired she truly was. That single moment — the moment she admitted the truth to herself — became the beginning of her healing.

She didn't need to change her life overnight.

She needed to stop lying to her own heart.

This is how self-return begins:

Not through revolution, but through honesty.

There was a man named Farhan who always felt a quiet pull toward a different path, yet he kept choosing the one others expected. One afternoon, while resting in a park, he allowed himself to imagine the life he truly wanted. Not the life he was told to build — the life that felt natural to him. That imaginary moment felt more real than all the years he spent forcing himself into a world that didn't fit him.

He realized then that his inner voice had never been silent.

He had simply been too busy living someone else's idea of success.

Returning to yourself is not about abandoning your responsibilities.

It is about including yourself in them.

It is about asking:

"Where am I in my own life?"

This question changes everything.

Because the truth is:

You can lose yourself slowly without realizing it.

You can drift away from your own needs.

You can forget who you were before fear shaped your choices.

You can silence the parts of you that once felt alive.

But you can also return.

At any age.

At any stage.

At any point in your story.

Every moment of honesty is a step back toward yourself.

When you admit what hurts, you stop carrying pain alone.

When you admit what you want, you stop settling unintentionally.

When you admit what you fear, the fear loses its power.

When you admit what feels wrong, you open the door to what feels right.

Your inner voice becomes louder every time you honor it.

People often ask, "How do I find myself again?"

The answer is simple:

You don't find yourself in the future.

You find yourself in the present — in the pieces of truth you allow yourself to feel today.

Returning to yourself is an ongoing journey.

Some days you will feel aligned.

Some days you will feel lost.

Some days your inner voice will speak clearly.

Some days it will feel faint.

But as long as you keep listening, you keep coming home.

Home to your emotional truth.

Home to your authentic desires.

Home to the life that feels meant for you.

Home to the person you were always meant to become.

By the end of this chapter, one thing becomes clear:

Your inner voice was never the problem.

Ignoring it was.

And now, you are learning to hear it again — softly, steadily, one honest moment at a time.

When you begin choosing truth over pretending, alignment over approval, peace over pressure, and authenticity over expectation, something magical happens:

You stop walking through life as a stranger to yourself.

You start walking with clarity.

With awareness.

With intention.

And most importantly, with yourself — finally, gently, fully.

CHAPTER 4: WHAT SHAPES OUR DIRECTION

PART 1: THE EARLY BELIEFS WE CARRY WITHOUT QUESTION

Long before we understand the world, we begin absorbing it.

And long before we choose our beliefs, certain impressions choose us.

These early beliefs become the quiet background of our lives.

We carry them without realizing it, trusting them simply because they arrived before we learned to question anything.

They become the lens through which we learn to see ourselves, others, and even God's plan for us.

Some beliefs are soft and comforting.

Some are heavy and unspoken.

Some are passed down lovingly.

Some are inherited unknowingly.

But all of them shape the beginning of our direction.

There was a boy named Aarav who grew up in a home where mistakes were treated gently. Whenever he stumbled, his mother reminded him, "Falling is part of learning." He didn't realize it then, but those simple words became one of the strongest foundations of his life. As he grew older, he faced challenges with an unusual sense of calm. He believed he could rise again because he learned early that falling wasn't failure — it was growth.

This early belief guided him silently.

It shaped his courage.

It shaped his persistence.

It shaped the way he interpreted struggle.

Not because someone taught him a rule, but because love planted a belief in him.

But not all early beliefs come from comfort.

There was a girl named Kavitha who grew up in a home where expressing emotions was seen as weakness. Over time, she learned to stay quiet, even when her heart was heavy. She believed that strength meant silence, that pain should be hidden, that vulnerability made her less deserving. She never questioned these beliefs because they were part of the environment she knew.

As she grew older, her inner world didn't match her outer world.

She had a gentle heart, but she lived behind a strong face.

She had deep emotions, but she buried them to appear "fine."

She longed for closeness, but her early belief told her closeness was risky.

This belief shaped her direction too — not toward God's peace, but away from her true path.

Early beliefs become powerful because they attach themselves to identity before the mind develops the ability to challenge them.

No child questions:

"Is this belief true?"

"Does this environment reflect who I really am?"

"Is this expectation meant for me?"

A child simply absorbs, accepts, and adapts.

These unnoticed beliefs become quiet laws we follow as adults.

- Some people believe they must always be strong, because they learned early that weakness wasn't allowed.
- Some believe they must always please others, because they grew up earning attention through obedience.
- Some believe love is unpredictable, because affection in their home came and went without explanation.
- Some believe they must not dream "too big," because no one around them dared to dream at all.
- Some believe they are not enough, simply because no one told them otherwise at the right time.

These beliefs do not come from truth.

They come from early impressions.

And yet, they shape the direction of a person's life more strongly than logic ever could.

This is where the deeper meaning enters —

because if God has already shaped your destiny, then the early beliefs placed around you were never accidental.

Even the difficult ones.

Even the confusing ones.

Even the painful ones.

Some early beliefs are given to strengthen you.

Some to teach you compassion.

Some to help you understand others more deeply.

Some to prepare you for a future only God can see.

Some to awaken wisdom later in life.

Your early environment does not define your destiny,

but it becomes the training ground for it.

The beliefs you accepted without question become the lessons you must understand later with awareness.

They become the inner signals that tell you when something feels wrong, even if you don't know why.

They become the emotional patterns you explore as you grow.

They become the quiet guidance that reveals where healing is needed.

The powerful thing is this:

You do not have to remain loyal to beliefs that limit you.

Awareness allows you to gently release the beliefs that were never yours to carry.

Understanding allows you to separate who you were taught to be from who you truly are.

Reflection allows you to see which beliefs were meant to guide you — and which were meant to be outgrown.

And in that process, your path becomes clearer.

Because once you understand the origins of your early beliefs,

you begin to understand the direction God always intended for you.

Not the direction shaped by fear.

Not the direction shaped by silence.

Not the direction shaped by survival.

But the direction shaped by truth, strength, and purpose —

the direction that was written for you long before you knew how to walk it.

PART 2: THE HIDDEN INFLUENCE OF OUR SURROUNDINGS

A person does not grow in isolation.

Every human being is shaped quietly by the spaces they live in — not just physically, but emotionally.

From childhood to adulthood, our surroundings become the unseen hands that shape our thoughts, our habits, our confidence, and even the way we interpret God's plan for us.

Most people don't realize how much influence their environment holds.

Because surroundings rarely speak loudly — they whisper.

They shape you gently, silently, consistently.

There was a boy named Reyansh who grew up in a home filled with encouragement. Every achievement, no matter how small, was acknowledged. Every effort was valued. Slowly, without anyone saying it directly, he learned to believe in himself. His surroundings gave him a sense of possibility. They taught him that trying mattered. They taught him that he could grow.

His confidence didn't come from a single moment — it came from thousands of tiny moments that shaped him without his awareness.

But not everyone grows in such environments.

There was a girl named Seerat whose home was always tense. Words were sharp. Expectations were heavy. Silence was filled with unspoken disappointment. She wasn't treated poorly, but the emotional tone of her home made her feel she had to be careful — careful with her words, her actions, her needs.

She brought this carefulness into adulthood.

She second-guessed herself even when she was right.

She apologized even when she wasn't wrong.

She hesitated even when she had the ability.

The environment she grew up in shaped her inner world long before she understood what inner worlds were.

This is how surroundings work.

They teach you things you don't realize you are learning.

Some homes teach courage.

Some teach fear.

Some teach independence.

Some teach silence.

Some teach confidence.

Some teach doubt.

Some teach love openly.

Some teach it quietly, or not at all.

And sometimes, surroundings shape direction by contrast —

by showing you what you do *not* want your future to look like.

There was a man named Adil who grew up around conflict. He watched arguments escalate often, and relationships break over small misunderstandings. For years, he feared he would repeat the same patterns. But as he matured, he understood that those surroundings didn't define him — they taught him what he wanted to rise above.

His environment didn't trap him.

It awakened a different kind of wisdom.

It shaped his direction by showing him the peace he longed for.

Surroundings influence a person in many ways:

- The conversations you hear
- The values you are exposed to
- The emotional tone of your home
- The habits of the people around you
- The dreams people talk about — or avoid
- The way love is expressed, or withheld
- The presence of encouragement
- The presence of pressure

These influences settle inside you quietly.

They become the background of your emotional world.

Understanding your surroundings matters because direction does not come only from destiny — it comes from interpretation.

And interpretation is shaped by environment.

For example:

If you grow up around fear, courage feels risky.

If you grow up around criticism, self-belief feels unrealistic.

If you grow up around chaos, peace feels unfamiliar.

If you grow up around stability, uncertainty feels threatening.

If you grow up around encouragement, dreams feel reachable.

The surroundings you experienced early in life help explain why certain choices feel natural to you and others feel uncomfortable.

But the important truth is this:

Surroundings may shape you, but they do not imprison you.

God uses experiences, environments, people, and places to prepare you — not to limit you.

Even difficult surroundings carry meaning.

They build resilience.

They build empathy.

They build understanding.

They build depth.

Some people grow beyond their environment with extraordinary strength.

Some transform because of what they experienced.

Some find purpose in contrast.

Some discover who they are by recognizing who they do *not* want to become.

And ultimately, every environment — good or difficult — becomes part of the path shaped for you.

Understanding this influence gives you clarity.

You stop blaming yourself for reactions you learned young.

You stop feeling confused about emotions that were shaped before you had control.

You stop judging yourself for habits formed in environments you didn't choose.

And with this understanding, something beautiful happens:

You begin choosing your own surroundings consciously.

You choose people who feel safe.

You choose places that bring peace.

You choose routines that nourish your inner world.

You choose environments that support your growth rather than suppress it.

Because once you realize how much surroundings shape direction,

you also realize you have the power to shape the surroundings of the future you want.

PART 3: THE UNSPOKEN RULES WE LEARN GROWING UP

Every childhood has its own set of unspoken rules — not written on walls, not taught in books, not said aloud, but absorbed quietly through repeated moments. These rules shape the way a person behaves long before they understand they have a choice.

These rules are powerful because they form early, at a time when the heart is soft, impressionable, and eager to belong.

And once they take root, they follow a person into adulthood, guiding decisions they don't even recognize as decisions.

Some unspoken rules sound like this:

"Don't upset anyone."

"Stay quiet; it's safer."

"Your feelings aren't important."

"Be strong; don't cry."

"Success equals worth."

"Don't ask for too much."

"Fit in, or you'll be left out."

"Love must be earned."

"Don't make mistakes."

None of these rules are spoken directly.

They are learned through tone, reactions, silence, expectations, and repeated patterns.

There was a boy named Ishan who grew up in a home where achievement was celebrated loudly, but emotional needs were met with quick solutions instead of understanding. Over time, he developed an unspoken rule:

"If I achieve enough, I will be loved enough."

No one told him this.

No one meant to give him this belief.

But the environment shaped it anyway.

He carried this rule into adulthood, working tirelessly, chasing milestone after milestone. But no matter what he achieved, he always felt he wasn't doing enough — not because achievements were lacking, but because the unspoken rule had wired him to believe that worth must be constantly proven.

This is the quiet power of childhood rules — they shape your sense of self even when you're unaware.

There was a girl named Aisha who grew up in a family where disagreements were avoided. Any hint of conflict was shut down quickly. She learned another unspoken rule:

"Silence maintains peace."

And so she grew into someone who held everything inside — her opinions, her hurt, her needs.

She kept peace outwardly, but inside she felt unheard.

Not because people refused to listen, but because she had learned early that her voice didn't belong in uncomfortable places.

Unspoken rules shape patterns:

- People who learned "don't cry" become adults who struggle to express pain.
- People who learned "don't fail" become adults terrified of trying.

- People who learned “don’t ask for help” become adults who suffer silently.
- People who learned “make everyone happy” become adults who forget their own happiness.
- People who learned “don’t take risks” become adults who feel stuck.

These rules don’t reflect God’s intention; they reflect early environments.

And understanding them is the first step toward breaking patterns that no longer serve your destiny.

There was a man named Dev who grew up being praised for being calm and easy-going. His unspoken rule became:

“Never be a burden.”

So he carried everything alone.

He didn’t cry in front of anyone.

He didn’t share his worries.

People admired him for being “strong,” but inside he was tired — not from life, but from carrying silent rules that denied him support.

It took him years to understand that the rule he lived by wasn’t truth — it was conditioning.

And once he recognized it, the weight he carried began to lighten.

Understanding your unspoken rules does not blame your upbringing.

It simply reveals the foundation from which you learned to interpret the world.

These rules shape:

— how you love

— how you trust

— how you dream

— how you fear

— how you react

— how you avoid

— how you seek comfort

— how you define success

— how you interpret God's signs

— how you decide what you "deserve"

Most people don't realize they are still living by rules that were meant for their 7–year–old self — not their adult self.

But here is the empowering truth:

Unspoken rules can be rewritten.

You can learn to say no even if you grew up believing you must always say yes.

You can express emotions even if you were taught to hide them.

You can dream boldly even if you were taught to stay small.

You can trust your feelings even if you were taught to ignore them.

You can choose peace even if chaos was familiar.

You can choose kindness for yourself even if you grew up being hard on yourself.

Awareness does not erase the rules.

But it gives you the power to decide which ones you want to keep.

And once you begin rewriting them, something shifts —

your direction becomes clearer,

your choices feel more aligned,

your path feels less inherited and more intentional.

Because you are no longer living by the rules of yesterday.

You are living by the truth of today —

a truth shaped not by childhood patterns,

but by the awareness God placed within you

so you could step into the life meant for you.

PART 4: HOW FEAR NUDGES US OFF OUR TRUE PATH

Fear is one of the most powerful forces in a person's life — not because it shouts loudly, but because it whispers quietly.

It doesn't always say, "Don't do this."

Sometimes it says, "Maybe later,"

or "You're not ready,"

or "What if you fail?"

or "What will they think?"

And without realizing it, those whispers begin shaping your direction more than any outer advice ever could.

Fear doesn't block destiny.

But it can delay your steps toward it.

There was a girl named Maya who always felt a quiet pull toward speaking her truth. She had strong emotions, deep thoughts, and a voice that could touch hearts. But every time she thought of expressing herself, fear appeared — soft, convincing, subtle. It told her:

"People will misunderstand you."

"They won't take you seriously."

"You might offend someone."

"Stay quiet. Stay safe."

So she did.

Years passed.

The words in her heart grew heavier.

But the day she finally allowed herself to speak — gently, honestly — she realized something profound:

the fear she carried wasn't protecting her; it was holding her back from the person she was meant to become.

This is how fear nudges us off our true path — not through dramatic blocks, but through quiet hesitation.

There was a man named Fahad who felt drawn toward building something of his own.

Whenever he imagined it, he felt alive.

But he also felt fear.

Fear of failure.

Fear of judgment.

Fear of losing stability.

Fear of disappointment.

So he stayed where he was — not because it was right, but because it was familiar.

Fear often disguises itself as logic.

It says, "Be practical."

It says, "Don't risk it."

It says, "Wait for a better time."

But deep inside, the heart knows when fear is disguising itself as wisdom.

There is a stiffness in the body, a tightness in the chest, a quiet sorrow that says:

"This isn't your true path."

Fear shows up in many forms:

- fear of being misunderstood
- fear of being judged
- fear of failing
- fear of succeeding
- fear of disappointing others
- fear of being abandoned
- fear of change
- fear of repeating past mistakes
- fear of losing comfort

- fear of being truly seen

These fears can silently redirect a person's entire life.

Not because God changed the path.

But because fear convinced the person to walk differently.

There was a woman named Tara who always dreamed of a peaceful, fulfilling life.

But every time she moved toward it, fear said:

"What if peace doesn't last?"

"What if you're not deserving of it?"

"What if you lose it?"

So she chose familiar chaos instead — not because she wanted it, but because she feared losing something she had never experienced.

Fear often pushes people away from what they deeply want.

But here is the important truth:

fear is not a warning that something is wrong — it is a sign that something matters.

Fear doesn't appear when you're walking the wrong path.

Fear appears when you are nearing a path that requires growth.

The heart knows this.

It feels the difference between danger and expansion.

But the mind, shaped by old wounds and past criticism, confuses the two.

Understanding your fear does not mean fighting it.

It means seeing it clearly.

Seeing that fear is often the echo of old beliefs.

Seeing that fear carries memories, not truth.

Seeing that fear protects the younger version of you, not the present one.

Seeing that fear appears when you're stepping into unfamiliar territory — often the territory where your destiny is waiting.

There was a boy named Aryan who once said something wise without realizing it:

"I'm not afraid of failing. I'm afraid of becoming the person I know I could be."

That sentence reveals everything.

Fear doesn't stop you because you are weak.

Fear stops you because your potential feels overwhelming.

But your potential is not an accident.

It is placed within you by God — long before you could understand it.

Fear is not a barrier.

It is a teacher.

It shows you where healing is needed.

It shows you where courage is waiting.

It shows you the exact places where your true path lies hidden.

When you start seeing fear this way, something shifts inside.

You no longer see fear as an enemy.

You see it as a signpost — pointing you toward the next chapter of your life.

And slowly, gently, you begin stepping in the direction that was always meant for you.

Not perfectly.

Not fearlessly.

But faithfully.

Because the path shaped for you is stronger than the fear inside you —

and your inner voice was never meant to be silenced by the echoes of yesterday.

PART 5: THE MOMENTS THAT SHAPE OUR SENSE OF WORTH

A person's sense of worth is not built in a day.

It is formed slowly, quietly, through moments that often feel too small to matter at the time.

Yet these moments become the emotional foundation on which we stand — or struggle — for years.

Some moments lift us.

Some moments break us.

Some moments strengthen us in ways we don't recognize until much later.

And many moments shape our direction more deeply than anything we consciously choose.

There was a boy named Samar who once received a simple compliment from a teacher:

"I believe in you."

It was only four words.

But for a child who often felt invisible, those four words became a source of courage.

Whenever he doubted himself, that memory returned like a soft light in a dark room.

This is how worth is built — through quiet, powerful moments of being seen.

But the opposite is true as well.

There was a girl named Nandini who grew up hearing casual criticism — not cruel, not intentional, but something like:

"Why can't you be more like your cousin?"

"Try harder; it's not enough."

"We expected better."

No one meant to hurt her.

But those small comments sank into her heart, shaping a belief she carried silently:

"I am always behind."

That belief affected the way she viewed opportunities, relationships, and even the blessings placed in her life.

She didn't realize that her sense of worth was built on tiny moments where she felt compared rather than understood.

This is the delicate truth:

The moments that affect our worth are rarely dramatic —

they're quiet, subtle, and deeply personal.

Worth is shaped by:

- the first time someone chooses you
- the first time someone ignores you
- the first time someone appreciates your effort
- the first time someone dismisses your feelings
- the first time someone believes in your dream
- the first time someone shames your mistake
- the first time someone protects your heart
- the first time someone breaks it

These moments become emotions.

Emotions become beliefs.

Beliefs become direction.

There was a man named Kabir who always put others 'needs before his own. He didn't do it for praise. He did it because the first time he ever received love as a child was when he helped someone.

So his unspoken belief became:

"I must serve to be valued."

This shaped his entire adult life.

He became generous, caring, dependable — beautiful qualities.

But hidden beneath them was a quiet fear:

“What if I stop giving? Will people still love me?”

Worth tied to performance is fragile.

Worth tied to comparison is painful.

Worth tied to approval becomes exhausting.

But worth tied to truth —

to who you are,

to the soul within you,

to the destiny God has written for you —

is steady, grounding, unshakeable.

Many people grow up internalizing moments that were never meant to define them.

A single harsh comment can overshadow years of kindness.

A single rejection can dim the memory of all the times you were chosen.

A single failure can erase the courage it took to try.

A single breakup can make you forget you are still worthy of love.

This happens because the heart remembers deeply —

especially in moments when it felt exposed.

But here is the gentle power of awareness:

Once you understand where your sense of worth came from,

you also understand that it can be rebuilt.

Worth is not fixed.

Worth is not given by others.

Worth is not defined by mistakes.

Worth is not determined by achievements.

Worth is your birthright —

a truth placed within you long before anyone had the power to influence your heart.

And the moments that once lowered your worth do not have the authority to shape your destiny unless you continue carrying them.

There was a woman named Sana who realized this in her late twenties. She remembered being laughed at during a school presentation. That moment made her believe she shouldn't speak in front of others. For years, she avoided every opportunity to lead, teach, or present.

But the moment she revisited that memory with adult eyes instead of a child's fear, she understood something profound:

She wasn't unworthy — she was simply young and learning.

The shame that shaped her path for years dissolved with understanding.

This is the beauty of self-awareness:

It returns your worth to its rightful owner — you.

When you begin to reclaim your worth:

You stop chasing validation.

You stop shrinking to make others comfortable.

You stop doubting your abilities.

You stop repeating patterns rooted in old wounds.

You begin listening more closely to the path God placed within you.

Because a person who knows their worth walks differently.

Not arrogantly, not loudly, but confidently —

with a calm understanding that their life has meaning,

their presence has purpose,

and their destiny is already held in divine hands.

PART 6: THE QUIET EXPECTATIONS WE INHERIT FROM OTHERS

Every person enters life with their own soul, their own nature, and their own destiny — yet along the way, people start carrying expectations that were never theirs to begin with. These expectations come quietly, often unspoken, woven into family traditions, societal norms, and the emotional atmosphere of childhood.

And before anyone realizes it, the expectations of others begin shaping the direction of a life meant to be guided from within.

There was a girl named Leena who grew up in a family that valued stability above all else. Every conversation about the future revolved around "security," "respect," and "safety."

No one ever forced her, but she absorbed the expectation:

"I must choose a predictable path to make everyone proud."

Yet inside, she longed for creativity, exploration, freedom.

Every time she considered a different life, a quiet voice inside whispered her truth —

but the louder voice was the inherited expectation she couldn't shake.

Her path wasn't chosen through clarity, but through loyalty.

This is what quiet expectations do.

They blur the line between what *you want* and what you *think you should want*.

There was a boy named Rohit who was always told he was "the responsible one."

At first, it felt like praise.

But as he grew older, it became pressure.

He believed he couldn't make mistakes.

He believed he must always stay strong.

He believed he must carry burdens silently.

The expectation wasn't spoken harshly; it was embedded softly.

And this shaped his entire adult behavior — until he realized he wasn't living his life, he was living the role others placed on him.

Expectations come in many forms:

- "Make the family proud."
- "Choose the safe option."
- "Be strong; don't show weakness."
- "Don't disappoint anyone."
- "Follow tradition."
- "Think practically, not emotionally."
- "Take care of others before yourself."
- "Success means stability."

None of these are necessarily wrong.

But when expectations override your inner truth, they become chains.

There was a woman named Diya who had a natural gift for empathy.

She felt deeply, understood quickly, and cared wholeheartedly.

Her environment saw this as a responsibility.

Even as a child, she was the one others leaned on.

So she inherited the expectation:

"Your needs must wait."

This became her habit in adulthood.

Her kindness was real — but her exhaustion was real too.

She didn't realize that she learned to prioritize others not because it was her nature,

but because it was her role.

Expectations shape direction subtly:

You choose careers that match what others imagined for you.

You stay in routines that feel familiar but unfulfilling.

You silence dreams because they don't align with "what makes sense."

You downplay emotions because the world taught you to appear strong.

You seek approval instead of meaning.

And slowly, without noticing, you drift away from the path God placed inside you.

But the moment you start examining these expectations, something shifts.

You begin to ask:

"Is this truly my desire or someone else's hope?"

"Do I want this life, or do I want to avoid disappointing people?"

"Am I choosing this path for love, or out of fear?"

"Is this expectation helping me grow, or keeping me small?"

Awareness doesn't break relationships.

Awareness breaks illusions.

And once the illusion breaks, something softer appears —

your own voice, your own wants, your own nature, your own direction.

Expectations inherited from others often come from good intentions.

Parents want safety.

Society wants stability.

Loved ones want predictability.

But only God knows the destiny designed for your soul.

And sometimes, the path written for you requires stepping beyond the expectations of those who love you.

There was a man named Sameer who once said:

“I spent so long trying to be the son they wanted, that I forgot the man I was becoming.”

When he finally listened to his own inner truth, he realized something profound:

He wasn’t rejecting his family —

he was reclaiming his life.

This is the gentle beauty of understanding expectations:

You can love people deeply without living their version of your destiny.

You can respect them fully without sacrificing your truth.

You can honor their hopes without abandoning God’s path for you.

When you begin walking with your own truth —

not out of rebellion,

not out of pride,

but out of awareness —

you step into a life that feels lighter, clearer, and more aligned.

Because destiny does not require perfection.

It requires honesty.

Honesty with yourself,

honesty with your heart,

honesty with the quiet direction placed inside you long ago.

And when you stop living for inherited expectations,

you finally begin living for the purpose meant for you.

PART 7: THE EMOTIONAL PATTERNS WE DON'T RECOGNIZE

Every person carries emotional patterns — responses that repeat themselves in different situations, with different people, at different times in life. These patterns are not random. They are learned. They are absorbed. They are shaped quietly through experiences you didn't fully understand when they first happened.

And because these patterns feel familiar, they often become invisible.

You don't notice them.

You don't question them.

You simply live inside them.

There was a man named Arjun who always felt anxious when someone raised their voice. He didn't know why. His adult mind told him he was fine, that nothing was wrong, that he shouldn't overreact. But his body responded before his thoughts could catch up.

His emotional pattern wasn't created in adulthood — it was created years earlier, in a home where raised voices meant danger.

Even though he grew up, the emotional memory stayed inside him.

Not to punish him — but because the heart remembers what shaped it.

This is how emotional patterns work.

They repeat themselves until they are understood.

There was a woman named Reeva who found herself choosing partners who didn't value her enough. Every relationship felt different at first, but somehow the ending always felt the same — she felt invisible, drained, unheard.

She began believing she was unlucky.

But in truth, she was repeating a pattern:

choosing emotionally distant people because distance felt familiar.

She had absorbed the idea that she must earn affection, not receive it naturally.

Her emotional pattern was not a flaw — it was a wound seeking recognition.

Many emotional patterns have similar roots:

- Shutting down during conflict because childhood taught you conflict is unsafe
- Pretending to be strong because expressing weakness was discouraged
- Choosing people who neglect you because that feels familiar
- Pushing people away because you're afraid they'll eventually leave
- Working endlessly because your worth once felt tied to achievement
- Feeling guilty for resting because productivity was praised more than peace
- Avoiding love because the past taught you that closeness brings pain
- Holding back emotions because being sensitive was once judged

These patterns do not arise from who you are —

they arise from what you lived through.

And the most powerful realization is this:

Emotional patterns do not reflect your destiny.

They reflect your history.

There was a boy named Zayan who struggled to accept compliments. Whenever someone praised him, he felt uncomfortable, almost suspicious. He didn't realize this came from years of hearing only criticism in his childhood. Praise felt unfamiliar — almost unsafe.

So he rejected it, not because he lacked confidence, but because he lacked experience receiving kindness.

Once he understood this, his entire inner world softened.

His emotional pattern loosened.

He began receiving the goodness life had been offering all along.

This is why understanding emotional patterns is essential:

You cannot walk toward your destiny while being pulled back by habits you don't understand.

When you begin recognizing patterns, you begin reclaiming freedom:

You notice when your reactions come from old wounds rather than current reality.

You stop blaming yourself for emotions that were learned, not chosen.

You stop repeating cycles that drain your spirit.

You stop confusing familiarity with truth.

You learn to respond from awareness, not habit.

There was a girl named Jiya who always apologized excessively.

Even when she wasn't wrong.

Even when she hadn't caused harm.

Even when she simply existed.

Her emotional pattern was shaped by years of being told, "Don't cause trouble," "Don't speak too loudly," "Don't be difficult."

Apologizing became her way of taking up less space.

One day, she realized she had outgrown the life that required her to shrink.

Her emotional pattern didn't match her destiny.

Her destiny required courage, voice, presence — not apology.

The heart carries old patterns as long as they feel necessary for survival.

But when life becomes safe, when awareness grows, when God gently leads you toward a larger version of yourself —

old patterns begin to fall away.

Not all at once.

Not perfectly.

But slowly, gently, through understanding.

Recognizing emotional patterns is not about blaming your past.

It is about freeing your future.

Because when you see your patterns clearly, you no longer move unconsciously.

You step into your life with intention.

You choose differently.

You feel differently.

You love differently.

You grow differently.

And slowly, you align with the direction that was always meant for you —

a direction shaped not by old wounds,

but by new awareness.

PART 8: THE INFLUENCE OF UNFINISHED STORIES

Every person carries unfinished stories inside them — moments that never found closure, emotions that were never expressed, memories that were never fully understood.

These stories don't disappear with time.

They settle quietly inside the heart, shaping the way you react, choose, trust, love, and fear.

Unfinished stories don't shout.

They whisper.

They appear in patterns, hesitations, longings, and sudden waves of emotion you cannot fully explain.

There was a woman named Tara who always felt nervous when someone raised their voice, even if they weren't angry at her. She didn't know why.

It wasn't until she reflected on her childhood that she remembered a moment — a moment where a raised voice once made her feel small and unsafe.

Her body never forgot.

Her heart never found closure.

This unfinished story continued to shape her present long after the moment had passed.

There was a boy named Samarth who avoided celebrations, even though nothing bad ever happened at them. He could never explain why crowded happiness made him uneasy.

Later in life, he remembered the day he shared good news as a child and was dismissed without acknowledgment.

His joy had once gone unnoticed, and that unfinished story taught him to hide happiness rather than risk being disappointed again.

This is how unfinished stories work —

they influence you silently, guiding your reactions without asking permission.

Some unfinished stories come from:

- love that ended without understanding
- apologies you never received
- apologies you never gave
- dreams you abandoned too quickly

- friendships that faded without closure
- harsh words that stayed in your memory
- emotions you were too young to process
- praise you needed but never heard
- moments of fear you never revisited
- unspoken grief
- unresolved guilt
- unexpressed love

The heart does not forget what the mind tries to move past too quickly.

There was a girl named Ira who always hesitated to trust people deeply. She wasn't cold; she was cautious.

Her unfinished story was simple — someone she loved once left without explanation.

And because she never understood why, her heart assumed closeness meant danger.

Unfinished stories are powerful not because they are dramatic,

but because they shape the meaning you attach to life.

They influence:

- what you avoid
- what you chase
- what you fear
- what you protect

- what you hide
- what you hope for
- what you doubt
- what you believe you deserve

Even when you think you've forgotten them.

There was a man named Yusuf who worked tirelessly, almost obsessively. People praised his dedication, but he knew the truth:

He was trying to silence an unfinished story —

a childhood memory where he was told he "would never achieve anything."

He wasn't working for success;

he was working to outrun a sentence spoken years ago.

A sentence that shaped the direction of his life more than he realized.

Unfinished stories often create two outcomes:

either we repeat them, or we fear them.

Some avoid love because love once hurt.

Some cling too tightly because they fear losing again.

Some avoid risks because a single failure created a lifetime of caution.

Some chase validation because they once felt unseen.

But here is the gentle truth:

An unfinished story is not your destiny.

It is simply a chapter waiting to be understood.

Awareness does not erase the past,

but it changes its power.

When you revisit a memory with understanding instead of fear,

it softens.

It loosens its grip.

It stops controlling your present.

There was a woman named Nisha who always pushed people away when they got too close.

Her unfinished story was a promise someone made and broke when she was young.

She didn't know that small heartbreak had shaped her adult relationships.

But the moment she saw the connection clearly, her heart breathed differently —

not healed completely, but lighter, freer, more aware.

Understanding unfinished stories allows you to walk toward the future without dragging the past behind you.

It does not mean rewriting history —

it means releasing the emotional weight you attached to it.

Because your destiny is not built from the moments that hurt you,

but from the meaning you give them once you understand them.

Every unfinished story carries a lesson,

a turning point,

a quiet truth about who you are

and who you are becoming.

And when you finally see that truth,

the path ahead becomes clearer —

not because the past disappears,

but because you are no longer walking blindly beneath its shadow.

You are walking with awareness.

With courage.

With understanding.

With the strength to continue the story rather than relive the same chapter.

PART 9: THE PEOPLE WHO CHANGE OUR DIRECTION WITHOUT KNOWING IT

Every person you meet leaves an imprint on your life — some soft, some heavy, some barely noticeable in the moment, yet deeply shaping in the long run.

People influence your direction silently, often without realizing the role they play in your journey.

Some people teach you what love feels like.

Some teach you what love should never feel like.

Some inspire courage.

Some awaken fear.

Some bring clarity.

Some create confusion.

Some push you forward.

Some break you in ways that eventually help you grow.

Not all people stay.

Not all people need to stay.

But every person becomes part of the map that guides you toward the path already written for you.

There was a girl named Rhea who once met a teacher who encouraged her curiosity. He didn't do anything extraordinary. He simply listened to her questions — something no one else had ever done with patience.

Years later, she realized that his quiet attention shaped her love for learning.

A simple human moment became a lifelong influence.

Then there was a man named Karan who fell deeply for someone who never treated him the way he deserved. The relationship drained him, confused him, and eventually broke something inside him.

Yet, it also showed him the painful truth of what he should never accept again.

The heartbreak shaped him — not through the love he received, but through the love he discovered he needed.

Some people teach you your value by failing to see it.

There was a boy named Ahaan who had a friend who constantly undermined him. The comments were subtle:

"You won't manage that."

"Don't aim too high."

"Someone else will do it better."

Over time, Ahaan absorbed this doubt. But one day, he met someone who believed in him effortlessly, genuinely. That contrast — between being doubted and being trusted — shifted the direction of his life.

Sometimes, you need to meet the wrong people to recognize the right ones.

Sometimes, you need to feel unseen to learn how deeply you deserve to be seen.

People influence your path in surprising ways:

- the mentor who opens your mind
- the friend who leaves without explanation
- the stranger who gives you courage
- the partner who teaches you your strength
- the critic who awakens your resilience
- the encourager who reminds you of your worth
- the competitor who pushes you to grow
- the quiet soul who listens when no one else does

Even brief encounters can leave lifelong impacts.

There was a woman named Meher who once comforted a stranger crying on a train. She thought it was a small gesture — just a moment of kindness. But years later, that stranger sent her a message saying that conversation stopped him from making a terrible decision.

Meher didn’t know she had changed someone’s direction.

Sometimes, we are shaping destinies we don’t know we’re touching.

Not all influences are gentle.

Some people hurt us so deeply that our entire path shifts.

But even those moments carry meaning — not because the pain was fair, but because the healing reveals strength we didn't know we had.

There was a boy named Viren who was betrayed by someone he trusted. For months, he couldn’t understand why it happened. But as time passed, he realized that betrayal pushed him toward people who valued loyalty deeply.

One painful ending led him toward healthier beginnings.

Life often moves us through people —

some who guide us,

some who challenge us,

some who leave too soon,

some who stay longer than expected,

some who reflect our wounds,

some who reflect our potential.

Each one plays a quiet role in shaping the direction God has already prepared for us.

Some people come to teach us patience.

Some come to teach us boundaries.

Some come to awaken desire.

Some come to reveal fear.

Some come to help us grow.

Some come to show us who we truly are.

Some come only to push us into the next chapter.

And some appear simply to remind us that destiny is not a straight line —

it is a path woven through human connection.

The most powerful realization is this:

People influence your life, but they do not control your destiny.

Their presence shapes you.

Their actions teach you.

Their departure redirects you.

Their love strengthens you.

Their mistakes awaken you.

But the path remains yours.

The direction remains yours.

The purpose remains yours.

And the destiny remains the one written for you long before any person entered your life.

Understanding this brings peace —

a calm acceptance that every person who touched your life, whether softly or painfully,

played a role in preparing you for the journey ahead.

PART 10: THE TURNING POINT WHERE WE BEGIN TO CHOOSE FOR OURSELVES

There comes a time in every person's life when the direction they've been following begins to feel unfamiliar — not because it is wrong, but because it no longer matches who they are becoming.

This moment is quiet.

It doesn't arrive with loud announcements or dramatic events.

It often appears in stillness, in reflection, or in a deep breath taken at the right time.

It is the moment a person realizes they have been living according to:

- early beliefs they never questioned
- surroundings that shaped their comfort
- unspoken rules they unconsciously followed
- fears they never examined
- emotional memories they carried for years
- expectations inherited from others
- patterns they didn't know they repeated
- unfinished stories that influenced their choices
- people who unknowingly shaped their path

And now, for the first time, they feel the need to choose consciously.

There was a man named Rohan who always lived by what others expected. He chose a career he didn't love, kept friendships that drained him, and avoided dreams he secretly longed for. But one morning, while sitting alone with a cup of tea, he felt a strange clarity — a recognition that his life looked "successful" but didn't feel meaningful.

He didn't quit everything that day.

He didn't take a dramatic step.

He simply acknowledged the truth:

"I have not been choosing for myself."

That recognition became the turning point.

This is how change begins — not with fireworks, but with honesty.

There was a woman named Zara who once believed she had to be strong all the time. She lived by this rule for years, never allowing herself to soften, rest, or ask for support. But one evening, after an overwhelming day, she cried quietly in her room.

Instead of feeling weak, she felt relieved — as if she had finally allowed herself to be real.

Her turning point wasn't about crying.

It was about realizing she didn't have to hold everything alone.

This moment of self-acknowledgment is where a new direction begins.

A direction chosen not out of fear, habit, approval, or expectation—

but out of truth.

The turning point often brings questions:

"What do *I* actually want?"

"How do *I* feel about this?"

“Whose voice have I been following?”

“Am I moving toward peace or away from myself?”

“Is this path mine, or inherited?”

These questions don’t create chaos —

they create clarity.

They bring a person back to themselves.

Back to the inner voice they ignored.

Back to God’s gentle guidance within them.

Back to the destiny already shaped for them.

There was a girl named Amara who always believed she had to be perfect. Her entire life was shaped around this hidden pressure. But one afternoon, while talking to a friend, she admitted something she had never said out loud:

“I’m tired of performing. I want to live.”

That confession changed her.

Not instantly, but gradually.

She began choosing things that felt true instead of impressive.

She began rejecting pressure instead of accepting it blindly.

She began living from authenticity rather than expectation.

Her turning point didn’t transform her life immediately —

but it transformed her direction.

This is the essence of a turning point:

It is the moment you stop running away from yourself and start walking toward who you were always meant to become.

When a person begins choosing consciously:

- Fear becomes smaller
- Inner peace becomes louder
- Patterns break
- Expectations loosen
- Boundaries strengthen
- Relationships become healthier
- Dreams feel reachable
- Faith becomes deeper
- The future feels clearer

Because decisions made from awareness carry a different energy —

an energy aligned with truth, not habit.

The turning point is not the end of struggle.

It is the beginning of understanding.

It is the moment you step out of autopilot and into awareness.

It is the moment destiny becomes visible.

It is the moment you stop living the life you were shaped into and begin living the life meant for you.

And in that shift — slow, gentle, honest —

a person finally sees the thread that connects everything:

The beliefs, the surroundings, the rules, the fears, the people, the stories, the memories…

they were not random.

They were preparing you.

Strengthening you.

Teaching you.

Guiding you.

So when the turning point arrives, you understand:

Nothing was wasted.

Nothing was meaningless.

Nothing was accidental.

It all led you to the moment where you finally choose the path written for your soul —

the path God designed long before you learned how to walk it.

CHAPTER 5: THE MOMENT DESTINY BECOMES CLEAR

PART 1: THE QUIET REALIZATIONS THAT CHANGE EVERYTHING

Life rarely changes in one big moment.

It changes in quiet realizations — soft, delicate shifts inside you that arrive without warning.

These realizations don't shout.

They don't demand attention.

They don't force you to act instantly.

Instead, they settle in your heart like a small light, showing you truths you overlooked for years.

There was a girl named Saanvi who always believed she was meant to follow a predictable path. Study, work, stability — nothing more, nothing less. But one evening, while sitting on her balcony after a long day, she felt a sudden clarity:

"This life is safe, but it isn't my life."

No dramatic event led to that moment.

No crisis, no heartbreak, no sudden change.

Just a quiet realization — one that shifted everything.

This is how destiny speaks.

Not through noise, but through a gentle awakening.

There was a man named Rehan who lived years ignoring his true interests because he believed they were impractical. But every few months, he felt a strange longing — a pull toward something else. He brushed it aside, thinking it was temporary.

One morning, while going through his usual routine, he felt a quiet sentence rise inside him:

“I cannot keep living on repeat.”

It wasn’t anger.

It wasn’t frustration.

It was truth — simple, calm, undeniable.

Quiet realizations are powerful because they come from the deepest part of you, not from fear, pressure, or expectation.

They come from the inner direction God placed within you — the direction that has been waiting patiently for you to notice it.

These realizations often appear in moments when you least expect them:

- in the middle of a routine
- during a long walk
- while talking to someone briefly
- during silence
- after a small disappointment
- after witnessing something simple
- or even while doing nothing at all

Clarity doesn’t always arrive when life is loud.

It arrives when your heart is finally calm enough to hear the truth.

There was a woman named Aaliya who stayed in a friendship that exhausted her. She kept trying, kept adjusting, kept forgiving more than she received. One afternoon, during a simple conversation, she suddenly felt something shift inside her — not anger, but recognition:

"I'm holding on to someone who let go long ago."

She didn't confront anyone.

She didn't cause chaos.

She simply understood.

And that understanding became her turning point.

Quiet realizations don't demand immediate action.

They simply reveal what has been hidden beneath noise, fear, habit, or hope.

These realizations can be subtle:

- "This is not who I am anymore."
- "I deserve better."
- "I cannot keep pretending."
- "This dream still lives in me."
- "I'm tired of being strong all the time."
- "I want something different now."
- "I can't keep living according to others."

They can be hopeful:

- "Maybe I'm capable of more than I thought."

- "Maybe things can change."
- "Maybe joy is possible for me."
- "Maybe this feeling is guiding me somewhere new."

They can be healing:

- "I don't need to carry this hurt anymore."
- "I am no longer the person who was wounded."
- "I can forgive myself."

And sometimes, they are spiritual:

- "God is preparing me for something."
- "This path was never random."
- "Everything makes sense in a way I couldn't see before."

Quiet realizations become the first soft step toward destiny.

They remind you that understanding doesn't always begin with answers — it begins with awareness.

Awareness of what hurts.

Awareness of what feels right.

Awareness of what no longer fits.

Awareness of what your soul has outgrown.

Awareness of where God is gently guiding you.

Some realizations feel like endings.

Some feel like beginnings.

But all of them create movement inside you.

And once that inner movement starts, no matter how slowly you walk,

you are no longer standing in the same place.

Because destiny doesn't reveal itself in a single moment.

It reveals itself in the quiet clarity that whispers:

"This is not the life I want to run from —

this is the life I'm finally ready to walk toward."

Part 2: When Life Pushes You Toward What You've Been Avoiding

Every person has something they quietly avoid — a truth they don't want to face, a dream they're afraid to chase, a conversation they postpone, a decision they keep delaying.

Avoidance feels safe in the beginning.

It feels familiar.

It feels easier than change.

But life has a way of nudging you forward, especially when the path you are avoiding is the very path meant for you.

There was a girl named Hana who always felt drawn toward a creative life, but fear kept her silent. She chose practical options, predictable routines, and safe steps.

Yet, every few months, life pushed her gently — a chance meeting with someone inspiring, an opportunity appearing unexpectedly, a feeling she couldn't ignore.

No matter how much she avoided it, the same direction kept returning.

Life does this.

It repeats the lesson until you're ready to learn it.

There was a man named Aarav who stayed in a job that drained him emotionally. He convinced himself that he couldn't leave, that stability mattered more than fulfillment.

But slowly, life began to push him.

Small discomforts grew into heavy exhaustion.

Tasks that once felt routine now felt unbearable.

He fell sick often, not because of the work, but because of the stress he refused to admit.

Life doesn't punish you.

It simply makes it harder to stay where you don't belong.

Avoidance is a form of delay — not protection.

Sometimes, what you avoid is exactly where your destiny is waiting.

Life uses subtle signals:

- unexpected dissatisfaction
- repeated setbacks
- restlessness at strange moments
- emotional heaviness
- opportunities appearing again and again
- old dreams resurfacing

- relationships shifting
- intuition becoming louder

These signals are not random.

They are guidance.

There was a woman named Roshni who avoided ending a relationship she knew wasn't right for her. She held on tightly, hoping time would fix everything.

But life gently kept pushing her — through growing distance, repeated misunderstandings, and the quiet ache of feeling unseen.

The moment she finally stepped away, she felt a peace that made her realize the truth:

She wasn't losing something.

She was making space for what she deserved.

Sometimes, life pushes you out of places you've outgrown long before you admit it.

There was a boy named Yusuf who avoided speaking up for himself. He hated conflict. He stayed silent even when his heart felt heavy.

Life pushed him in small ways — moments where staying silent caused more pain than speaking the truth.

Eventually, he realized that avoiding discomfort was costing him his voice.

This is the gentle wisdom:

What you avoid usually reveals what you fear the most —

and what you fear the most often holds the key to your growth.

Destiny is not a straight line.

It bends, curves, stops, and restarts.

But it also persists.

And when you resist your path, life redirects you.

Sometimes softly.

Sometimes firmly.

Sometimes repeatedly.

But always with purpose.

There was a woman named Raina who kept avoiding a career change she longed for. She stayed because of comfort, familiarity, and predictability.

But life kept whispering:

"You are meant for more."

And those whispers became louder each time she ignored them.

Finally, she reached a moment where staying felt more painful than leaving.

That was the moment she knew — life had been guiding her all along.

Avoiding something doesn't make it disappear.

It simply delays the clarity waiting for you on the other side.

Life pushes you toward what you avoid because:

- your heart is ready
- your soul has outgrown the old chapter

- your destiny needs you to step forward
- you deserve more than your fear allows
- you cannot stay small in a life built for growth

And here is the deeper truth:

God does not allow you to stay where your spirit is shrinking.

So life nudges.

And nudges again.

Until you move.

Not because you are being punished,

but because the path ahead holds more peace, purpose, and alignment than the place you are clinging to.

Avoidance delays destiny —

but destiny waits patiently,

and life keeps guiding you back to where you are meant to be.

PART 3: THE SIGNS THAT KEEP APPEARING FOR A REASON

Life has a subtle way of repeating the things you need to notice.

A feeling you've tried to ignore.

A thought that returns at unexpected moments.

A dream that refuses to fade.

A message you hear from different people in different places.

A situation that keeps repeating itself.

These signs are not accidents.

They are reminders.

They are guidance.

They are gentle signals pointing you toward something meant for your life.

There was a girl named Meera who always felt drawn toward a certain path — not because it was comfortable, but because it felt right in a way she couldn't explain.

Every time she stepped away from it, life brought her back:

a conversation with a stranger,

a sudden opportunity,

a repeated thought during quiet moments,

a feeling she couldn't shake.

The signs were small, but they were persistent.

She realized eventually that the direction she kept returning to wasn't random —

it was meant for her.

This is how signs work.

They don't force you.

They guide you.

There was a man named Sameer who didn't believe in "signs" at all.

He was logical, practical, grounded.

But when he felt unhappy at work, he noticed the same theme appearing everywhere — articles about career change, advice from friends, unexpected discussions about passion, even dreams at night.

The same message kept following him.

Not loudly, but consistently.

Until one day he admitted:

“I think life is telling me something.”

Signs don’t always appear as big events.

Most of the time, they come in soft patterns:

- The same idea returning again and again
- The same emotion arising in different situations
- A repeated longing you push away but cannot forget
- A strange comfort when you think about a certain path
- A deep discomfort when you stay in the wrong place
- People entering your life at the exact moment you needed clarity
- Opportunities appearing repeatedly
- Unexpected coincidences that don’t feel random

There was a woman named Anya who kept seeing a particular quote everywhere:

“Sometimes, what you’re afraid of is what will set you free.”

She saw it on social media, heard it in a conversation, noticed it in a book.

After the third time, she realized it wasn’t coincidence —

it was a message she needed to face.

It pushed her toward a decision she had been delaying.

Signs are gentle invitations.

They guide without pressure.

They remind without demanding.

And they appear repeatedly because humans often ignore the first whisper.

Sometimes a sign appears as peace.

Sometimes it appears as discomfort.

Sometimes as a person.

Sometimes as a moment.

Sometimes as a repeated thought that returns no matter how many times you dismiss it.

Signs don't come from fear.

They come from truth.

Fear shouts.

Truth whispers.

And those whispers come back until you listen.

There was a boy named Eshan who kept encountering the same lesson in different relationships — the lesson that he needed to set boundaries.

He didn't want to accept it.

He avoided conflict.

But life repeated the message through different people, different situations, different disappointments.

Each time, the pattern became clearer.

Each time, the sign became harder to ignore.

Life will repeat the message until you learn the lesson.

Sometimes, signs appear through contrast —

when something feels wrong, so you realize what is right.

When someone treats you poorly, so you learn your worth.

When a situation closes, so you understand it was never meant for you.

And sometimes, signs appear through hope —

the warmth you feel about a dream,

the excitement you feel about a possibility,

the calmness that settles in your heart when you imagine a different path.

The signs are not outside you alone —

they are within you too.

When destiny becomes clearer, the signs around you begin to align with the signs inside you.

You start feeling:

- "This path feels right."
- "I can't ignore this anymore."
- "Something is guiding me."
- "This keeps coming back for a reason."
- "I'm meant to pay attention to this."

Signs don't reveal the whole path.

They only reveal the next step.

But that next step is enough.

Enough to shift your direction.

Enough to guide your heart.

Enough to move you closer to the life meant for you.

Because the signs that repeat are not coincidences —

they are reminders from life,

whispers from within,

and gentle nudges from the destiny already written for you.

PART 4: WHEN YOUR HEART OUTGROWS YOUR OLD LIFE

There comes a moment — gentle, quiet, but unmistakable — when your heart no longer fits inside the life you once lived comfortably.

It doesn't mean something is wrong.

It simply means you are growing.

Growth is not always loud.

Sometimes it feels like a soft restlessness.

Sometimes like a gentle ache.

Sometimes like a feeling that your old life is too small for who you're becoming.

There was a girl named Kavya who always followed the same routine. It was familiar, predictable, and safe. But slowly, she began feeling a strange distance from her own life — as if she was watching herself from the outside.

Nothing bad happened.

She simply realized she wasn't excited anymore.

She wasn't learning, she wasn't expanding, she wasn't alive in the way she once hoped to be.

This was her heart whispering:

"You have outgrown this chapter."

Outgrowing an old life is not betrayal.

It is evolution.

There was a man named Nitesh who stayed in a friend circle he had known since childhood. They shared memories, history, laughter — but as he matured, he noticed something shifting. Their conversations no longer nourished him. Their jokes no longer felt like home. Their expectations no longer matched his spirit.

He didn't love them any less.

He simply realized he had grown in a different direction.

Sometimes distance isn't a sign of conflict.

It is a sign of growth.

The heart expands silently.

It grows through experiences, awareness, pain, healing, and truth.

And as it expands, it becomes harder to shrink yourself back into old versions of life that once felt comfortable.

This inner shift appears in many forms:

- when you feel drained by routines that once felt normal
- when conversations that once entertained you now feel empty
- when familiar places no longer give you peace
- when you crave deeper meaning rather than distraction
- when your dreams begin pulling you stronger than your fears
- when the person you're becoming no longer matches the life you're living

There was a woman named Zoya who stayed in a job she didn't enjoy. It wasn't terrible — it just didn't speak to her soul.

Every day felt the same.

Every goal felt distant.

Every achievement felt hollow.

One morning, she woke up and realized something simple yet powerful:

"I'm not unhappy. I'm unfulfilled."

This realization changed everything.

Outgrowing your life is not about sadness.

It is about awareness.

Sometimes you outgrow:

- people
- habits
- environments

- dreams
- beliefs
- roles
- versions of yourself you once worked hard to build

And that is okay.

It means you are moving toward the direction meant for you.

There was a boy named Farhan who lived for years trying to meet expectations given to him by others. When he finally began listening to his inner voice, he felt guilty — almost disloyal — for wanting something different.

But with time, he learned:

You are not meant to stay in places that no longer nourish your growth.

Outgrowing a life does not mean the old life was wrong.

It simply means it served its purpose.

People change.

Hearts evolve.

Souls deepen.

Destiny reveals itself slowly.

As you grow, the life you once fit into may become too tight, like clothing you've worn for too long.

It doesn't fit because you've expanded.

Not physically — internally.

And when this happens, you face a powerful truth:

Staying the same becomes harder than changing.

You feel it emotionally.

You feel it spiritually.

You feel it in the way your heart responds to life.

And the moment your heart outgrows your old life, something inside you begins to shift:

- You want clarity instead of comfort.
- You want meaning instead of approval.
- You want truth instead of routine.
- You want connection instead of noise.
- You want growth instead of stagnation.

These desires are not random.

They are signs that destiny is becoming clearer.

They are reminders that you cannot shrink to fit a life that was meant to be temporary.

Outgrowing your old life is not the end —

it is the beginning of the life that was always waiting.

The moment you accept that you have outgrown a chapter,

you make space for the chapter written for the person you are becoming.

PART 5: THE INNER CALM THAT COMES BEFORE BIG DECISIONS

Before every major turning point in life, there is a moment of inner calm — a stillness that settles quietly inside you, even if everything around you feels uncertain.

This calm doesn't look dramatic.

It doesn't come with confidence or loud motivation.

It often feels like a soft exhale after years of holding your breath.

It is the calm of clarity.

The calm of acceptance.

The calm that arrives when your heart finally stops arguing with your truth.

There was a girl named Mira who struggled for years to decide whether she should leave a job that drained her. She thought she needed a sign, a push, a perfect moment.

But the clarity didn't come through external events.

It came one morning when she woke up and felt peaceful about the thought of moving on.

Not excited.

Not fearless.

Just peaceful.

That peace was her signal — the quiet approval that she was ready.

Big decisions are rarely made through sudden confidence.

They are made through a steady calm that grows inside you.

There was a man named Kabir who spent months debating whether to distance himself from a relationship that no longer felt healthy. Fear held him for long, and confusion clouded his thoughts.

But one day, during a normal evening, he felt something he hadn't felt in a long time:

stillness.

He realized he wasn't afraid anymore.

He wasn't angry anymore.

He wasn't overthinking anymore.

He simply felt done — gently, silently, truthfully.

This inner calm is often the final step before change.

People assume big decisions require certainty.

They don't.

They require honesty.

And honesty creates calm.

Inner calm appears when:

- you've outgrown a situation
- your heart is ready, even if your mind is scared
- you stop fighting what you already know
- you release guilt and accept reality
- you trust that life is guiding you gently
- the decision aligns with who you are becoming

This calm doesn't erase fear.

It exists alongside it.

But it is stronger than fear.

Fear makes noise.

Calm speaks truth.

There was a woman named Sana who always made decisions through pressure and worry. But the biggest decision of her life — moving to a new city — came through quiet certainty.

She wasn't sure how things would work out.

She didn't have a perfect plan.

But every time she imagined the new chapter, she felt light.

And whenever she imagined staying, she felt heavy.

Lightness is the language of inner calm.

Heaviness is the language of resistance.

Life becomes clearer when you learn the difference.

Inner calm is not passive.

It is a sign of alignment — your heart, mind, and path moving in the same direction.

Sometimes this calm arrives days before making a decision.

Sometimes minutes.

Sometimes months.

But it always arrives right before you step into the life meant for you.

This calm is not created by logic.

It emerges when you finally accept the truth you've been avoiding.

And the moment this calm settles inside you, the decision feels less like a risk and more like a release.

A release from:

- self-doubt
- confusion
- pressure
- fear
- guilt
- old versions of yourself

Big decisions don't require certainty about the future —

they require clarity about the present.

And that clarity speaks through calm.

When you feel this inner calm, you don't need validation from others.

You don't need approval.

You don't need guarantees.

You just know — quietly, softly, deeply — that the step ahead is yours to take.

Because the path you are moving toward isn't chosen out of fear or pressure.

It is chosen out of alignment.

And alignment always feels like peace.

This is why, before destiny becomes clear, the heart becomes still.

Not silent — still.

Not numb — steady.

That inner calm is God's way of telling you:

"You're ready now."

PART 6: THE INVITATIONS LIFE GIVES YOU TO BEGIN AGAIN

Life doesn't always rebuild itself through big, dramatic moments.

Most of the time, new beginnings enter gently — like soft invitations, subtle opportunities, or small openings that appear just when your heart becomes ready.

These invitations don't force you.

They call you.

They whisper rather than shout.

They appear as possibilities that feel strangely comforting, even if they're unfamiliar.

There was a girl named Naina who spent years feeling stuck in the same routine. She felt disconnected, tired, and unsure of her next step.

But one day, she received a small opportunity — a short workshop invitation.

Nothing major.

Nothing life-changing on the surface.

Yet, attending it opened a door inside her that had been closed for years.

Life often sends small invitations first.

It tests your readiness gently.

There was a man named Imran who went through a difficult breakup. For months, he felt empty. The world seemed quiet and heavy.

Then one afternoon, he met someone unexpectedly at a café — not a romantic encounter, but a simple conversation that reminded him he could connect again.

It wasn't a new relationship.

It was an invitation back into life.

Life doesn't always replace what you've lost.

Sometimes it simply reminds you that you are still capable of feeling.

Invitations appear in many forms:

- a new idea that excites you
- a conversation that sparks curiosity
- a chance to try something unfamiliar
- a shift in the people around you
- a moment of unexpected courage
- an opportunity that comes back twice
- a feeling that says, "Maybe I can start again"
- or even a gentle inner nudge you can't explain

These invitations are not coincidences.

They are signs that your soul is ready to turn a page.

There was a woman named Rhea who always wanted to switch careers but never had the confidence. One morning, while scrolling online, she saw a small announcement for a beginner's course in the field she secretly loved.

She almost ignored it.

But something inside her whispered, "Just try."

She listened to that whisper.

And that simple choice became the doorway to a new chapter.

Every new beginning starts with a moment like this —

small, quiet, ordinary, but meaningful.

Life gives invitations in cycles:

When you lose something, life invites you to rediscover purpose.

When you feel empty, life invites you to seek meaning.

When you feel stuck, life invites you to step forward.

When you outgrow your surroundings, life invites you to move.

When you heal, life invites you to open your heart again.

And when destiny becomes clearer, life invites you to walk toward it.

There was a boy named Aditya who always dreamed of studying abroad. He dismissed the idea for years, believing it was too unrealistic.

But one day, he received a message from an old acquaintance who had done exactly that — sharing their experience casually.

That one conversation reignited his dream.

It wasn't guidance.

It wasn't pressure.

It was an invitation — a reminder of what still lived inside him.

New beginnings are often hidden inside simple moments.

But the truth is:

Life only invites you to begin again when you're emotionally ready — not when you're perfect, not when everything is stable, but when your heart has grown enough to move forward.

Your readiness is not measured by confidence.

It is measured by willingness.

A willingness to try.

A willingness to explore.

A willingness to trust again.

A willingness to believe that something new is possible.

And once you accept even one small invitation, life responds.

More openings appear.

More clarity comes.

More courage grows.

More peace settles.

This is the beauty of the process:

Beginnings don't come from forcing change.

Beginnings come from noticing the gentle invitations life places in front of you —

and choosing, even softly, to step toward them.

Because every invitation you accept brings you closer to the path meant for you.

Closer to the person you are becoming.

Closer to the destiny waiting quietly inside your heart.

PART 7: WHEN LETTING GO BECOMES THE ONLY WAY FORWARD

There comes a moment in every person's life when holding on feels heavier than releasing — not because you stopped caring, but because your heart outgrew what once felt right.

Letting go isn't a sign of weakness or failure.

It is an act of truth.

A quiet admission that a chapter has reached its natural end.

There was a woman named Aditi who stayed in a friendship long after the connection faded. She kept trying, kept adjusting, kept hoping it would feel like before.

But one day, during a simple conversation, she felt something shift — not anger, not hurt, just clarity:

"I don't belong here anymore."

She didn't walk away immediately.

She simply accepted the truth.

And acceptance was the first step toward letting go.

Letting go is not always dramatic.

Most of the time, it begins with a tired heart.

There was a man named Rishabh who held on to a dream he created when he was much younger. He kept chasing it because he didn't want to feel like he had wasted years.

But with time, he felt disconnected from it.

His heart no longer recognized the dream that once excited him.

One evening, while reflecting alone, he whispered a sentence he had been avoiding for years:

"I'm allowed to change."

Letting go is often not about the other person or the old dream —

it is about releasing the version of yourself that no longer exists.

Letting go becomes necessary when:

- your heart feels tired, not challenged
- a place feels heavy instead of comforting
- you keep giving but receive nothing in return
- the old dream no longer reflects who you are
- the person you're becoming doesn't fit your past roles
- the relationship survives only through effort, not connection
- the situation demands losing yourself to keep it
- staying feels more painful than leaving
- your soul feels quiet when you think of moving on

- your inner peace grows when you imagine a different life

Letting go is not leaving something behind —

it is making space for what aligns with your future.

There was a girl named Myra who kept holding on to someone who wasn't ready to love her. She convinced herself that patience was strength.

But slowly, her own joy faded.

Her laughter quietened.

Her spirit dimmed.

One afternoon, she felt something she hadn't felt in months:

lightness —

not because something changed, but because she finally understood she deserved more.

Letting go does not come from anger.

True letting go comes from clarity.

Clarity that says:

"This is not my path anymore."

"My heart deserves peace."

"I cannot grow here."

"This version of my life has completed its purpose."

"I am losing myself by staying."

Letting go becomes easier when you realize that holding on doesn't fix anything —

it only delays what life is trying to teach you.

Sometimes God closes a door gently.

Sometimes life removes what you would never remove yourself.

Sometimes your heart loses interest in what once mattered because you are being prepared for something new.

Letting go is not losing.

Letting go is trusting.

Trusting that your life is not ending —

a deeper chapter is beginning.

There was a boy named Veer who held onto guilt from his past mistakes. No matter how much he tried to move forward, he kept pulling himself back by replaying old moments.

One day, he finally told himself the truth:

“I have punished myself long enough.”

And that moment of forgiveness became his freedom.

Letting go is not always about people.

Sometimes it's about:

- releasing a version of yourself
- releasing pressure
- releasing guilt
- releasing old habits
- releasing self-doubt
- releasing memories that no longer serve you

Letting go becomes the only way forward when staying still hurts more than moving ahead.

And the moment you let go — truly let go — something beautiful happens:

Your heart becomes lighter.

Your mind becomes clearer.

Your path becomes visible.

Your spirit begins to breathe.

And life begins to open again.

Because letting go is not the end of your story.

It is the moment destiny begins to move freely in your life —

without resistance, without fear, and without the weight you once carried.

PART 8: THE GENTLE COURAGE HIDDEN INSIDE YOU

Courage is often imagined as something loud — bold decisions, dramatic actions, fearless leaps.

But the courage that shapes your life rarely looks that way.

Most of the time, real courage is quiet.

Soft.

Unseen.

It appears in moments when no one is watching, when your heart is trembling, when you take a step even though uncertainty surrounds you.

There was a woman named Aisha who always believed she was timid. She thought courage belonged to people who were confident, outspoken, unshakable.

But when life pushed her toward changes she feared, she discovered something new —

not bravery in the way she expected,

but a gentle courage that whispered:

“Just try.”

She didn’t roar.

She didn’t rush.

She simply took one small step forward.

And sometimes, that is the purest form of courage.

Gentle courage doesn’t erase fear —

it moves with fear.

There was a boy named Kunal who wanted to pursue a passion that felt unrealistic. His family encouraged stability, his mind warned him about risk, and his fear reminded him of past failures.

But still, every evening, he found himself researching, dreaming, imagining.

That persistence was courage —

quiet, consistent, and alive.

Courage often hides in your smallest actions:

- getting out of bed on a difficult day
- telling someone the truth

- admitting you're hurting
- choosing to rest instead of running
- applying for something you think you won't get
- saying "no" when your heart needs it
- walking away from what isn't right
- trusting someone again
- giving yourself another chance

People underestimate these moments, yet they are the moments that shape destiny.

There was a girl named Ritu who stayed silent for years because she feared judgment. One day, she finally opened up to a trusted friend about her struggles.

Her voice shook.

She cried.

She hesitated.

But she spoke.

That single conversation became the turning point of her healing.

A soft act of courage changed the direction of her life.

Gentle courage appears when:

- your inner voice grows louder than your fear
- you feel the pain of staying the same
- life pushes you toward growth
- you realize you deserve better

- you trust yourself even slightly
- you are tired of pretending
- you feel ready to begin again, even if you're uncertain

Gentle courage doesn't come from confidence.

It comes from truth.

It arrives when something inside you whispers:

"I can't keep living like this."

or

"I want something more."

or

"I am ready to try."

This courage grows quietly.

It grows through heartbreak, healing, patience, reflection, and self-awareness.

There was a man named Arnav who carried guilt for years. He believed he wasn't worthy of happiness because of one mistake he made long ago.

His courage was not in forgetting the past —

but in forgiving himself for it.

Letting yourself heal is a courageous act.

Letting yourself dream again is courageous.

Letting someone love you after being hurt is courageous.

Letting yourself leave a place that no longer feels like home is courageous.

Courage doesn't always look like strength.

Sometimes it looks like softness.

Sometimes it looks like honesty.

Sometimes it looks like taking a small step in a new direction with shaking hands.

Your gentle courage is the quiet force that keeps your life moving forward, even when you don't realize it.

And here is the beautiful truth:

You have always been braver than you think.

You have survived moments that once felt impossible.

You have carried pain that would have broken others.

You have kept going even when your heart felt tired.

The courage inside you is not loud — but it is steady.

It is woven into your character, your growth, your decisions, your dreams.

When destiny becomes clear, courage doesn't suddenly appear.

Destiny simply awakens the courage that was always there.

And that gentle courage is enough —

enough to take the next step,

enough to trust the unknown,

enough to build a life aligned with your truth.

PART 9: HOW PAIN CLEARS THE PATH FOR PURPOSE

Pain is one of the most misunderstood experiences in life.

People often see it as a sign that something has gone wrong —

a failure, a punishment, a misstep, a weakness.

But pain is often the moment life becomes honest.

It strips away illusions, breaks false attachments, and reveals truths that comfort never could.

Pain forces you to see what you tried to ignore.

And in doing so, it clears the path for purpose.

There was a girl named Zaina who stayed in a relationship that drained her, hoping things would improve. She ignored the early signs, dismissed her discomfort, and convinced herself to hold on.

But when heartbreak finally came, she felt shattered.

At first, she thought the pain meant she had lost something precious.

But as she healed, she realized the pain had removed what was blocking her growth.

Pain didn't destroy her life —

it freed her from a path that wasn't meant for her.

This is how pain works:

It breaks what is false so truth can enter.

There was a man named Aarush who always followed a career chosen for him, not by him. He pushed himself relentlessly, ignoring his exhaustion and inner emptiness.

Eventually, the stress caught up to him. He fell sick, and for the first time in years, he had to pause.

That pause — forced by pain — made him question the life he was living.

It was the first time he asked himself:

“Is this really my path?”

Pain didn’t appear to punish him.

It appeared to redirect him.

Pain often arrives with a message:

- “You are not where you need to be.”
- “Something in your life needs to change.”
- “You are outgrowing this version of yourself.”
- “You are ignoring the truth inside you.”

Pain is not the enemy.

Avoiding it is.

There was a woman named Kiara who carried childhood wounds that shaped her entire adult life. She built walls, avoided closeness, and pretended she didn’t need anyone.

But loneliness eventually broke through those walls.

The pain she tried to outrun became the pain that finally helped her heal.

Sometimes the pain you avoid is the pain that saves you.

Pain clears the path for purpose by:

- removing people who are not meant to stay
- showing you your worth through loss
- revealing the truth in relationships
- forcing you to confront emotional patterns
- breaking routines that no longer serve you
- pushing you out of comfort that limits your growth
- making you more compassionate and understanding
- opening your heart to change
- awakening strength you didn't know you had

Pain softens what stubbornness cannot.

It clarifies what confusion hides.

It releases what your heart clings to out of fear.

There was a boy named Vihaan who lost a job he thought was everything. He felt devastated. But months later, he found an opportunity that aligned perfectly with his strengths.

Looking back, he realized something powerful:

The loss wasn't the end — it was the beginning.

Pain didn't remove his purpose.

It removed what stood in its way.

Life often shifts through discomfort.

You grow through the moments you didn't choose but had to face.

The breaking moments become the making moments.

Pain teaches you to let go.

Pain teaches you to begin again.

Pain teaches you what truly matters.

Pain teaches you who truly cares.

Pain teaches you who you really are.

Most importantly, pain teaches you that you are far stronger and more resilient than you ever believed.

What feels like the worst moment often becomes the doorway to the best chapter.

Not because the pain disappears,

but because it transforms you.

Pain doesn't define you.

It refines you.

It removes what isn't meant for your future

so that you can walk toward your purpose with clarity, humility, and strength.

And when you look back, you realize something sacred:

The pain you once prayed to escape

was the very thing that guided you to the life meant for you.

PART 10: THE MOMENT YOU FINALLY TRUST THE LIFE MEANT FOR YOU

There comes a time in every person's life when fear becomes quieter, doubt becomes softer, and trust begins to grow — not suddenly, but naturally.

This trust doesn't come from knowing the future.

It comes from understanding the journey that brought you here.

When you look back and see how every detour taught you something,

how every heartbreak shaped your strength,

how every loss redirected your path,

how every sign appeared at the right time,

and how every quiet realization guided you gently —

you begin to trust the life meant for you.

Not because you finally have all the answers,

but because you finally see the pattern.

There was a woman named Tara who spent years fighting her own fears. She questioned every decision, doubted every step, and feared every change.

But one day, while sitting quietly after a difficult month, she felt a strange peace — a soft acceptance inside her.

She realized that every time she took a step forward, life supported her in unexpected ways.

This was the moment she understood:

"I don't need to know everything.

I just need to trust the direction."

Trust grows slowly, but once it arrives, it transforms everything.

There was a boy named Ishaan who always tried to control every detail of his life. He believed safety came from certainty. But the more he tried to control, the more life surprised him with unexpected shifts.

Eventually, he learned that some paths are not meant to be planned — they are meant to be walked.

And when he let go of control, something beautiful happened:

his heart relaxed for the first time in years.

Trust doesn't remove uncertainty.

Trust allows you to walk through uncertainty with calmness.

The moment destiny becomes clear isn't when you see the whole future —

it's when you feel safe taking the next step.

Trust appears when:

- you stop forcing outcomes
- you stop holding onto things that drain you
- you stop fearing new beginnings
- you stop doubting your worth
- you start listening to your inner calm
- you start recognizing signs
- you start believing life is guiding you
- you start understanding that what is meant for you will not pass you
- you start realizing you're stronger than your past

Trust isn't blind.

It is built from everything you've lived through.

There was a girl named Noor who faced many setbacks — plans failing, friendships ending, doors closing. For years, she wondered why everything felt so difficult.

But later, when she stepped into a chapter that felt right in every way, she realized the truth:

"If the earlier paths had opened, I would have missed the one meant for me."

Trust often comes from hindsight.

Pain gives clarity.

Clarity gives understanding.

Understanding gives trust.

When you finally begin to trust the life meant for you, something shifts inside you:

- you stop rushing
- you stop fighting yourself
- you stop comparing your journey
- you stop doubting your timing
- you stop fearing endings
- you stop forcing connections

Instead, you start moving with ease —

even when things aren't perfect.

Even when the path is uncertain.

Even when you feel vulnerable.

Because trust whispers something fear never does:

"You are not walking alone."

There was a man named Advay who once said:

"I don't know where I'm going, but I finally trust the One who is guiding me."

That sentence held more strength than any detailed plan he ever made.

This is the moment destiny becomes clear —

not when everything makes sense,

but when you feel aligned with where life is taking you.

You begin to see meaning where you once saw chaos.

You begin to see protection where you once saw loss.

You begin to see preparation where you once saw delay.

You begin to see purpose where you once saw pain.

This trust frees your heart.

It allows you to breathe deeply.

It allows you to walk confidently.

It allows you to live fully.

Because when you trust the life meant for you,

you no longer fear what's next —

you welcome it.

You understand that every chapter has purpose,

every shift has meaning,

every person has a role,

every setback has a lesson,

and every moment — even the difficult ones —

moves you closer to the life designed for you.

Trust is not the end of the journey.

It is the beginning of walking with peace.

And when trust settles in your heart,

you finally step into your destiny —

not with fear,

not with doubt,

but with quiet confidence that you are exactly where you are meant to be.

CHAPTER 6: REGRET AND THE RETURN TO YOURSELF

PART 1: THE REGRET THAT FINALLY WAKES YOU UP

Regret doesn't come loudly.

It doesn't arrive with sudden chaos or dramatic realizations.

It often enters your life quietly — through a thought that lingers longer than usual, a moment that feels heavier than it should, or a memory that suddenly stings in a way it never did before.

Regret is the feeling that tells you:

"I could have chosen differently."

And even though it hurts, it also wakes you up.

There was a girl named Riddhi who stayed in situations that didn't honor her worth. At the time, she didn't realize she was shrinking herself. She believed patience was strength, silence was peace, and loyalty was love.

Years later, she looked back and felt a heavy ache — not because she had failed, but because she abandoned her own needs for too long.

That ache was regret.

And that regret became her turning point.

Regret is not a punishment.

It is awareness arriving late.

There was a man named Ayush who ignored his dreams for years because he feared judgment. He convinced himself that practicality mattered more than passion. But whenever he saw others living boldly, something inside him tightened.

He wasn't jealous — he was regretful.

Regretful that he had treated his own desires as if they were unimportant.

Regret often forms around the things you didn't do:

- the words you didn't say
- the boundaries you didn't set
- the love you didn't protect
- the dreams you didn't chase
- the signs you ignored
- the truth you avoided
- the risks you didn't take

Regret reveals where your heart wished it had been braver.

There was a woman named Tia who realized too late that she had given people more chances than they deserved. She stayed long after her heart had begun breaking, hoping her loyalty would repair what wasn't meant to be repaired.

When she finally walked away, she felt regret — not for leaving, but for not leaving sooner.

This is how regret wakes you up:

It shows you where you stayed small, quiet, or scared.

Regret is painful because it holds a truth you once weren't ready to see.

But here is the part people often overlook:

Regret is a sign of growth.

It appears only when you've become wise enough to see your past clearly.

When you regret something, it means:

- you've changed
- you've learned
- you've outgrown your old choices
- you're ready to choose differently
- your heart has matured
- your soul wants better for itself

Regret is the first crack in the old version of you.

A soft break that lets light enter.

Most people fear regret, but regret is not the end.

Regret is the beginning of becoming aware.

It wakes you up gently.

It says:

"Now that you know better, you can do better."

Regret does not exist to make you suffer.

It exists to remind you that you are capable of more.

More honesty, more courage, more growth, more alignment with the life meant for you.

When regret wakes you up, you don't have to fix the past.

You only have to stop repeating it.

This is where transformation begins —

not in perfection, but in awareness.

And sometimes the deepest healing begins with the simplest sentence:

“I should have chosen myself earlier.”

PART 2: SEEING WHERE YOU STAYED TOO LONG OR TRIED TOO HARD

One of the hardest truths to face is recognizing where you stayed longer than you should have — not because you were weak, but because you cared deeply, hoped honestly, and believed things would change.

Regret grows quietly in the spaces where your heart kept giving long after it stopped receiving.

There was a woman named Ishita who stayed in a friendship that no longer felt like home. She gave chances, made excuses, and adjusted her needs again and again.

At the time, she thought she was being loyal.

But years later, she looked back and felt a soft ache:

“I kept trying long after the connection ended.”

This realization didn’t make her foolish.

It made her human.

Every person has a place in their life where they tried too hard —

for love, for approval, for belonging, for peace.

There was a man named Dev who stayed in a job that drained him because he didn't want to disappoint anyone. He convinced himself that stability was enough.

But every night, he felt a quiet heaviness he couldn't explain.

Only later did he understand that he wasn't tired of work —

he was tired of forcing himself to fit into a life he had outgrown.

Regret often comes from seeing the gap between what you accepted and what you deserved.

It surfaces when you finally see:

- where you kept giving without balance
- where you stayed out of fear rather than love
- where you lowered your standards for temporary comfort
- where you silenced your voice to keep peace
- where you ignored the signs your heart already understood
- where you worked harder than the situation ever deserved
- where you tried to fix what wasn't meant to be yours

Regret shines a light on the places where your effort was sincere, but misdirected.

There was a boy named Arin who tried endlessly to impress people who never valued him. He adapted himself in every way possible — his personality, his dreams, even his quiet preferences — hoping someone would finally see his worth.

Years later, when he matured emotionally, he realized something painful and freeing:

“I was trying to earn a place I already deserved without changing myself.”

Seeing where you tried too hard can feel heavy at first.

But this heaviness is not guilt —

it is understanding.

Understanding how much your heart endured.

Understanding how deeply you loved.

Understanding how strongly you held on.

Understanding how fear kept you in places meant only for one chapter of your life, not your whole story.

There was a girl named Neha who stayed in a situationship she knew wasn’t real. She gave effort, compassion, patience — everything except the one thing she truly needed: honesty with herself.

When it finally ended, regret flooded her.

But as she healed, she saw the truth:

She wasn’t wrong for wanting love.

She was only wrong for hoping someone else would eventually offer what she kept giving.

Regret does not say, “You were foolish.”

Regret says, “You have learned.”

Seeing where you stayed too long teaches you:

- your loyalty is strong
- your intentions were pure

- your heart is capable of deep commitment
- you deserve balance, not one-sided effort
- your younger self did the best they could
- you know better now — and will choose differently

Trying too hard does not make you wrong.

It makes you someone who believed in possibility.

Someone who gave their best.

Someone who had hope.

But once you see it clearly, you cannot unsee it.

And that clarity becomes your turning point.

You no longer pour your energy into places that drain you.

You no longer fight for people who don't meet you halfway.

You no longer mistake effort for love.

You no longer stay just because you're afraid of leaving.

That is the quiet power of regret:

it reveals where you lost yourself so you can find yourself again.

When you finally see the places where you stayed too long or tried too hard, you don't blame your past —

you understand it.

You grow from it.

And you walk forward with a softness that says:

"I know my worth now."

PART 3: WHEN YOU REALIZE YOU DESERVED BETTER ALL ALONG

One of the most powerful turning points in a person's life is the quiet moment they finally understand — truly understand — that they deserved better than what they settled for.

Better treatment.

Better honesty.

Better effort.

Better love.

Better respect.

Better peace.

This realization doesn't come suddenly.

It arrives slowly, tenderly, often after a long period of confusion or hurt.

But when it comes, it changes everything.

There was a girl named Anaya who always accepted the bare minimum from people she cared about. She convinced herself that small crumbs of affection were enough, that patience would eventually be rewarded.

Years later, she looked back and felt a sharp clarity:

"I kept asking for so little because I believed that's all I was worth."

That understanding broke her heart —

and healed it at the same time.

Regret shifts the moment you realize your past wasn't a reflection of your worth —

it was a reflection of what you believed about yourself at that time.

There was a man named Reyansh who spent years trying to impress people who never truly cared. He shaped himself according to their expectations, thinking acceptance required effort, silence, and sacrifice.

But one day, during a casual conversation, he felt a sudden truth settle inside him:

"I am worthy of being valued without performing for it."

This was the moment he understood he deserved better —

not from others, but from himself.

Realizing you deserved better is painful because it forces you to see:

- how much you tolerated
- how much you minimized your feelings
- how often you stayed quiet
- how deeply you gave without receiving
- how long you waited for someone to change
- how much you settled for less than respect
- how often you abandoned your own needs
- how far you strayed from your own truth

But this realization is also liberating.

It marks the moment your heart returns to itself.

There was a woman named Mehek who kept chasing closure from someone who repeatedly hurt her. She thought understanding their reasons would help her heal.

But the clarity arrived not from them, but from within:

"If someone wanted to respect me, they already would have."

She didn't need answers anymore.

She needed self-respect.

And that realization became her freedom.

When you finally understand that you deserved better all along, regret begins to transform:

It stops blaming.

It starts understanding.

It stops hurting.

It starts healing.

It stops weighing you down.

It starts lifting you up.

Because regret is no longer about what happened.

It becomes about what you now know —

and what you will never again accept.

There was a boy named Aarav who always apologized first, even when he wasn't wrong. He feared losing people more than losing himself.

But as he grew older, he recognized a truth he had ignored for years:

“Anyone who genuinely values me would never want me to suffer alone.”

This realization changed how he treated himself.

It taught him that self-respect is not distance — it is clarity.

When you realize you deserved better, you begin to:

- speak more honestly
- protect your peace
- choose yourself
- walk away earlier
- trust your intuition
- set higher standards
- stop begging for effort
- stop shrinking to fit
- stop forcing connections
- stop confusing loyalty with self-sacrifice

You begin to understand that wanting better was never the problem —

accepting less was.

This shift is gentle but life-changing.

It is the beginning of emotional maturity.

It is the moment your past stops dictating your future.

It is the moment you honor who you are instead of what you've been through.

And perhaps the most healing realization of all is this:

You didn't deserve better because of what you did.

You deserved better because of who you are.

You always did.

You just couldn't see it then.

PART 4: UNDERSTANDING YOUR YOUNGER SELF WITH COMPASSION

At some point in the journey through regret, a softer realization begins to appear—

a realization that your younger self wasn't foolish, weak, or unaware.

They were simply doing the best they could with the understanding they had at that time.

And when you see this clearly, judgment fades.

Compassion takes its place.

There was a boy named Siddharth who used to blame himself for staying in a painful chapter far longer than he should have. He replayed memories endlessly, wondering why he didn't leave earlier, speak up sooner, or choose differently.

But one evening, while looking at an old photo of himself, something gentle shifted inside him.

He didn't see a boy making bad decisions.

He saw someone trying — someone hopeful, unsure, and scared to lose people he loved.

He finally whispered to himself,

"I forgive you. You didn't know better."

This is the moment regret starts healing.

Your younger self wasn't trying to ruin your life.

They were trying to survive.

They were trying to love.

They were trying to belong.

They were trying to make sense of feelings that were too big for a heart not yet mature.

There was a girl named Tara who blamed herself for trusting the wrong people. For years, she felt embarrassed for how much she gave, how much she hoped, and how deeply she believed.

But when she grew emotionally and looked back, she realized something important:

Her trust wasn't a mistake.

It was a sign of her pure heart.

She didn't make bad choices because she was naive.

She made them because she had never been taught what real love or respect looked like.

Compassion allows you to understand your past self without shame.

It lets you see:

- why you stayed
- why you tried too hard
- why you silenced your feelings

- why you accepted less
- why you ignored signs
- why you tolerated what hurt
- why you feared leaving
- why you repeated old patterns

Not because you were weak —

but because you were young, hopeful, loyal, and still learning.

There was a woman named Karishma who blamed herself for years for not choosing her own dreams. She followed the path others expected because she believed approval meant security.

Only later did she understand that her younger self was not choosing out of fear, but out of love — a desire to keep peace, to avoid disappointment, to fulfill expectations.

Once she saw this, regret softened.

Compassion grew.

Understanding your younger self means recognizing:

- they didn't have your current strength
- they didn't have your present clarity
- they didn't have the wisdom pain has now given you
- they didn't know they deserved better
- they didn't know how to let go
- they didn't know how to listen to their inner voice

They were learning.

And learning is never shameful.

There was a boy named Aman who once said,

"If I met my younger self today, I wouldn't scold him. I would hug him."

Because he realized that the person who needed forgiveness the most was the one who kept trying, failing, and trying again — without guidance, without experience, and without the understanding he has now.

Compassion is the bridge between regret and healing.

It transforms regret from:

"I can't believe I did that,"

into

"I understand why I did that."

Compassion allows you to take ownership of your past and still be gentle with yourself.

It frees you from punishing yourself for decisions made with a different level of awareness.

And most importantly, compassion reminds you that every part of your journey — even the mistakes — helped shape the wisdom you now carry.

Your younger self didn't ruin your path.

They walked you to the doorway of growth.

Their choices led you to clarity.

Their heartbreak gave you strength.

Their confusion gave you understanding.

Their hope kept you going.

And now, with compassion, you can finally say:

"Thank you for trying. I'll take it from here."

PART 5: YOU CANNOT REWRITE THE PAST, BUT YOU CAN REWRITE YOURSELF

There comes a point in every healing journey when you realize that no amount of thinking, replaying, or wishing can change what has already happened.

You cannot go back and choose differently.

You cannot warn your younger self.

You cannot erase past decisions or undo old heartbreaks.

But you *can* rewrite the person you are becoming.

And that truth carries more power than the past ever did.

There was a man named Arjun who spent years wishing he could go back and fix the mistakes he made in his early twenties. He regretted every choice that led him toward pain, every moment he stayed silent, every dream he abandoned.

But with time, he understood something important:

His past was unchangeable.

But his future was not.

He could not rewrite the story behind him,

but he could rewrite the story ahead of him.

This realization is where transformation begins.

Regret loses its weight the moment you understand that its purpose is not to chain you to the past —

but to guide your future.

There was a woman named Leher who often said,

“I wish I had known better.”

But when she reflected deeper, she realized the true meaning:

If she *had* known better, she would have chosen better.

The fact that she can see her mistakes now means she has grown enough to choose differently going forward.

That growth is the rewriting.

You cannot rewrite:

- the people you trusted
- the words you didn’t say
- the opportunities you missed
- the love you gave to the wrong person
- the time you wasted
- the boundaries you didn’t set
- the signs you ignored

But you *can* rewrite:

- the people you allow into your life now
- the way you speak your truth today
- the opportunities you create for yourself
- the love you choose moving forward

- the time you value from this day onward
- the boundaries you protect
- the signs you finally pay attention to

Your past choices shaped you, yes —

but they do not have the power to limit who you can become.

There was a girl named Nidhi who carried guilt for years because she stayed in a painful situation far too long. She wished she could go back to tell her younger self to walk away earlier.

But one day she asked herself a different question:

"If I had walked away earlier, would I have the strength I have now?"

Her answer changed her perspective.

Her pain had pushed her into wisdom.

Her regret had shaped her awareness.

Her past had not been wasted — it had been a teacher.

This is the deeper truth:

Your past cannot be rewritten, but its meaning can.

Regret becomes wisdom when you allow it to change:

- how you love
- how you choose
- how you speak
- how you protect your heart
- how you trust yourself

- how you move toward your future

Every lesson you learned shapes the person you are building now.

And that new version of you —

the wiser one,

the calmer one,

the clearer one —

is the one who will create the life your younger self never knew how to choose.

You cannot undo your past,

but you can honor it by becoming someone stronger than your mistakes.

You can rewrite yourself by:

- choosing with intention
- listening to your inner voice
- respecting your emotional needs
- trusting the wisdom earned through pain
- walking away when something feels wrong
- valuing your peace more than approval
- believing you deserve better
- building a life that reflects your truth

This is the freedom regret offers when you understand it deeply:

It stops being a weight and becomes a map.

It points you toward the person you are meant to be.

It pushes you to rise above who you once were.

It invites you to step into your next chapter with strength instead of fear.

You cannot change the path behind you.

But you can choose every step ahead.

And those steps — the ones made with clarity, courage, and self-respect —

will rewrite your entire life in ways your past could never limit.

PART 6: TURNING REGRET INTO DIRECTION

Regret often feels like a heavy weight, but beneath that weight lies something powerful — clarity.

Clarity about what hurt you, what limited you, what drained you, and what no longer belongs in your future.

Once you see this clearly, regret stops being a reminder of what you lost and becomes a guide toward what you need.

Regret becomes direction the moment you ask:

"What is this feeling trying to teach me?"

There was a woman named Sana who regretted trusting someone who repeatedly took advantage of her kindness. For months she blamed herself, wondering why she didn't walk away sooner.

But when she began to reflect, she discovered the real message behind her regret:

She wasn't regretful because she trusted —

she was regretful because she ignored her own discomfort.

That realization changed everything.

From that day on, she promised herself she would never silence her intuition again.

Her regret became her inner compass.

This is how direction is born —

not from guilt, but from understanding.

There was a man named Ishaan who regretted missing an opportunity that could have changed his life. But instead of drowning in "what if," he asked himself,

"What was I afraid of then?"

The answer surprised him:

He wasn't afraid of failure.

He was afraid of being seen.

That insight became his direction —

to stop hiding when something mattered to him.

Regret points toward the areas of your life that need attention:

- the dreams you abandoned
- the boundaries you didn't set
- the people you tolerated
- the silence you kept
- the chances you didn't take
- the love you didn't give yourself
- the truth you avoided

- the moments you denied your worth

These are not wounds —

they are signposts.

Regret teaches you what you truly value.

What you truly desire.

What you truly need.

What you never want to repeat.

What you should protect next time.

What parts of your heart need healing.

And what direction your life is quietly calling you toward.

There was a girl named Mahi who regretted how much time she spent trying to please others. She gave her energy to people who didn't appreciate it and shaped her life around keeping everyone comfortable.

But when she saw how empty that left her, regret transformed into direction.

She began choosing people who valued her.

She began choosing peace over approval.

She began choosing a life she didn't have to shrink inside.

Her regret didn't break her.

It redirected her.

Turning regret into direction means understanding that:

- your past choices were part of your learning

- your pain sharpened your awareness
- your mistakes revealed your needs
- your heartbreak clarified your worth
- your hesitation taught you courage
- your silence taught you the importance of voice

Every regret is a lesson wrapped in emotion.

When you unwrap the lesson, you gain direction.

Regret says,

"I wish I had acted differently."

Direction says,

"I will act differently from now on."

Regret says,

"I should have protected myself."

Direction says,

"I will protect myself now."

Regret says,

"I stayed too long."

Direction says,

"I know when to leave."

Regret says,

"I ignored my truth."

Direction says,

"I will honor my truth moving forward."

The moment regret becomes direction, something shifts inside you —

you start living consciously instead of repeating old patterns.

Your choices become intentional.

Your boundaries become stronger.

Your relationships become healthier.

Your dreams become clearer.

Your heart becomes steadier.

You stop walking in circles around your past.

You start walking in a straight line toward your future.

Because regret is not meant to punish you.

It is meant to guide you.

And once you understand its message, regret becomes a quiet strength —

a reminder that every misstep helped shape the person who is now ready for a better, clearer chapter.

PART 7: BECOMING THE PERSON YOU ONCE NEEDED

There comes a moment in the journey through regret when you finally understand something powerful —

your past wasn't meant to break you.

It was meant to shape you into the person your younger self desperately needed.

You become wiser through what confused you.

You become stronger through what hurt you.

You become clearer through what misled you.

You become softer through what overwhelmed you.

You become aware through what once blinded you.

And this transformation is not sudden.

It grows quietly, gently, through every regret you've carried and every lesson you've learned.

There was a woman named Raina who always wished someone had protected her when she was younger — someone who would have taught her boundaries, encouraged her dreams, and reminded her she was worthy.

For years she searched for that person in others.

Only later did she realize the truth:

She was becoming that person for herself.

She became the voice she never heard.

She became the strength she never had.

She became the comfort she once begged for.

She became her own turning point.

This is what healing does —

it turns you into the person you once needed the most.

There was a boy named Aarav who regretted how often he doubted himself. He wished someone had believed in him earlier, someone who had told him that his dreams mattered.

But as he grew, life revealed something meaningful:

Belief didn't need to come from outside.

It needed to come from within.

And slowly, he became the version of himself who believed —

not out of pride, but out of understanding.

Becoming the person you once needed means:

- you speak up when your younger self stayed silent
- you choose peace over approval
- you listen to your intuition
- you protect your heart
- you honor your needs
- you walk away earlier
- you love yourself deeper
- you trust your path
- you give yourself patience
- you show yourself compassion

It means you no longer abandon yourself the way you once abandoned your inner voice.

There was a girl named Arushi who once longed for someone to tell her she was enough — just as she was. She waited for years to hear those words from people who didn't know how to offer that kind of love.

Now, whenever she faces doubt, she tells herself gently,

"You are enough."

And this simple sentence heals the wounds created by years of silence.

Becoming the person you needed doesn't mean you ignore your past.

It means you rise above it.

It means you use what you learned to build the version of yourself who can finally live with clarity, confidence, and calm.

Regret may have been part of your journey,

but it is not your identity.

Your identity is found in who you become because of regret —

not in the mistakes themselves.

Every lesson reshaped you.

Every heartbreak softened you.

Every disappointment strengthened you.

Every wrong turn redirected you.

Every regret taught you how to choose better next time.

And now, standing at this point in your life, you carry something your younger self never had:

- wisdom
- awareness
- understanding
- emotional strength
- clarity of direction

- the courage to walk a new path

This is the real victory —

not avoiding mistakes,

but growing so deeply that those mistakes become the foundation for the life you're about to build.

When you become the person you once needed,

you don't just heal —

you transform.

You no longer chase love; you create it within.

You no longer fear endings; you understand their purpose.

You no longer cling to the wrong people; you choose better connections.

You no longer lower your standards; you rise to meet your truth.

You no longer hide your voice; you trust it.

And most importantly,

you finally return to yourself —

not the old self,

not the wounded self,

but the wiser self who knows how to walk toward the future with grace.

Regret guided you here.

Understanding lifted you.

Compassion healed you.

Direction strengthened you.

And now, in this final part, you step into the most important chapter of your journey:

Becoming the person you needed —

and the person you were always meant to be.

CHAPTER 7: WALKING TOWARD THE LIFE MEANT FOR YOU

PART 1: THE SHIFT FROM SURVIVING TO LIVING

There comes a moment in life when you realize you've spent years simply trying to make it through each day — waking up, moving forward, carrying your responsibilities, holding your emotions together, and doing your best to stay afloat.

You weren't living; you were surviving.

Survival makes you strong, yes —

but it also makes you numb.

It teaches you how to endure, not how to feel.

How to continue, not how to grow.

How to protect yourself, not how to receive what life wants to offer.

There was a girl named Esha who spent most of her early twenties trying to be "fine." She buried her disappointments, rushed through her days, and ignored her inner exhaustion.

One evening, after a long week, she sat down and realized she couldn't remember the last time she felt genuinely alive.

Not busy.

Not distracted.

Alive.

That moment became her turning point.

The shift began — quietly, softly, naturally.

Survival ends the moment awareness begins.

There was a man named Veer who spent years in a routine that drained him. Every day felt the same — predictable, heavy, dull. But one day, while walking home, he noticed the sunset. Not because it was extraordinary, but because he finally had the space inside him to notice something beautiful.

It was such a small moment.

But for him, it was a sign he was waking up from years of emotional autopilot.

Living begins with noticing —

noticing your feelings, your needs, your limits, your desires.

It begins with allowing yourself to breathe without rushing.

Allowing yourself to slow down.

Allowing yourself to feel the fullness of life again.

The shift from surviving to living happens when:

- you stop numbing your emotions
- you stop running from your truth
- you stop forcing yourself into old patterns
- you stop pretending everything is fine
- you stop accepting a life that doesn't feel like yours

And instead, you begin to:

- listen to your inner voice
- honor your feelings
- choose what nourishes you

- let go of what drains you
- trust the small signals guiding you forward
- open your heart again
- give yourself permission to grow

There was a woman named Ira who once said,

“I didn’t realize how long I had been holding my breath until life finally gave me space to exhale.”

This is what the shift feels like —

a slow, gentle release.

A quiet exhale after years of tension.

Living doesn’t begin with big decisions.

It begins with small awakenings.

A moment of clarity.

A spark of interest.

A new boundary.

A peaceful morning.

A single honest thought.

And slowly, you realize something profound:

You are not the same person who entered the past chapters of your life.

You are wiser now.

You are clearer now.

You are ready to live, not just survive.

This shift is the first step toward the life meant for you.

It signals that your inner world is finally ready — ready to choose with intention, ready to walk with awareness, ready to experience life with depth instead of defense.

This is where alignment begins.

This is where purpose starts to unfold.

This is where the new version of you quietly steps forward.

PART 2: LISTENING TO THE PULL OF YOUR INNER DIRECTION

Once you stop merely surviving, something subtle begins to awaken inside you — a quiet pull, a gentle nudge, a sense that something in your life is trying to guide you toward a new path.

This pull isn't loud or dramatic.

It doesn't force you.

It invites you.

It feels like a soft knowing, a quiet instinct, or a small spark of curiosity that keeps returning, no matter how many times you try to ignore it.

There was a boy named Yuvraj who always felt a subtle restlessness whenever he thought about his future. For years, he dismissed it as confusion.

But as he grew emotionally, he realized that restlessness wasn't confusion —

it was direction.

A signal that something in his life was waiting to be explored.

Inner direction doesn’t shout.

It whispers.

It whispers through:

- the thought that won’t leave you
- the feeling that something is missing
- the urge to try something new
- the discomfort of staying where you are
- the excitement you feel for no obvious reason
- the peace that appears when you imagine a different version of your life

These whispers are not random.

They are guidance.

There was a woman named Naina who stayed in a job that offered stability but not fulfillment. Every now and then, she imagined a different path — one that felt more meaningful.

She pushed the thought away each time, believing it was unrealistic.

But the thought kept returning.

This is how inner direction works:

It returns until you acknowledge it.

Listening to the pull of your inner direction doesn’t mean you must change everything at once.

It simply means you begin to pay attention.

You notice the patterns.

You notice the feelings.

You notice what brings you peace.

You notice what drains your spirit.

You notice where your energy rises and where it collapses.

There is wisdom in what your heart gravitates toward —

and there is truth in what it pulls away from.

Inner direction becomes clearer when:

- you stop forcing yourself into spaces that don't feel right
- you stop pretending your needs don't matter
- you stop silencing your intuition
- you stop ignoring small discomforts
- you stop choosing based on fear
- you stop denying your own voice

And instead, you begin to:

- follow your curiosity
- trust the feelings that repeat
- choose what nourishes you
- take small steps toward what feels aligned
- explore possibilities without fear of failure
- let your inner voice guide the next decision

There was a girl named Kavya who said,

"I used to think my confusion meant I was lost. Now I understand it was my heart pushing me toward something better."

She didn't have a full plan.

She didn't need one.

All she needed was the courage to follow what felt right.

Inner direction rarely reveals the entire path.

It reveals the next step.

You won't always know where the road leads,

but you will know when a certain direction feels true —

because your heart responds differently.

Your mind may argue,

your fears may protest,

your doubt may interrupt—

but your inner direction stays steady.

It shows itself in moments of peace.

It strengthens in moments of honesty.

It grows in moments of awareness.

And slowly, you begin to trust it.

Because the pull you feel is not random.

It is your life calling you forward.

It is your growth asking for space.

It is your truth trying to speak.

It is the beginning of alignment.

When you listen to that pull — even softly —

your steps begin to match who you are becoming,

not who you once were.

And this is the moment life starts shifting around you.

PART 3: THE PEOPLE AND OPPORTUNITIES THAT ARRIVE WHEN YOU ALIGN

Life has a quiet intelligence.

It senses when you are ready for something new, even before you do.

And the moment you begin aligning with your inner direction — even in small ways — life responds in ways that often feel surprising, comforting, and strangely timed.

People arrive just when you need them.

Opportunities appear without being forced.

Paths open that were once blocked.

Moments seem to fit together as if they were designed for you.

It doesn't happen because the world suddenly changes —

it happens because *you* change.

There was a girl named Rhea who spent years feeling disconnected from her dreams. But when she finally began taking small steps toward what felt right, she met someone unexpectedly — a mentor who saw potential in her that she had forgotten existed.

They crossed paths by chance, but the timing wasn't accidental.

It was alignment.

Alignment attracts what confusion keeps away.

There was a man named Zaid who always felt stuck, surrounded by people who didn't understand his journey. But as he began listening to his inner direction — choosing healthier spaces, clearer boundaries, and honest conversations — new people entered his life.

People who respected him.

People who understood him.

People who spoke the same emotional language.

People who matched his growth, not his wounds.

This is the quiet magic of alignment:

The right people walk in when the wrong people walk out.

Opportunities also shift.

Doors that once felt locked begin to loosen.

Ideas that once felt impossible become practical.

Paths that once felt hidden become visible.

Not because your luck changes —

but because your energy does.

When you align internally, you naturally attract what fits your spirit.

Alignment brings:

- conversations that open your mind
- people who help you grow
- chances that feel "meant to be"
- clarity about your next steps

- connections that feel effortless
- guidance that arrives right on time
- opportunities that match your strengths
- support you didn't know you needed

Life always had these things for you —

you just weren't in the emotional place to receive them.

There was a woman named Aakriti who used to force everything — friendships, plans, timelines, relationships. But when she began living from her inner truth instead of fear, something softened.

She stopped chasing.

She started choosing.

And suddenly, things began to fall into place on their own.

People who once overlooked her started respecting her.

Opportunities she once doubted herself for began seeking her instead of the other way around.

This is the shift that alignment creates:

You stop forcing.

You start flowing.

You stop begging for space.

You start belonging naturally.

You stop trying to be chosen.

You start choosing yourself — and life responds.

There was a boy named Samar who once said,

"The moment I stopped pretending, the world started meeting me halfway."

And he was right.

Life meets you where you meet yourself.

When you align:

- you become clearer
- your energy rises
- your choices strengthen
- your boundaries sharpen
- your courage grows
- your stability deepens

And because of that, the world begins offering you things that reflect your inner state.

People who match your growth.

Opportunities that match your purpose.

Moments that match your readiness.

Nothing forced.

Nothing rushed.

Nothing confusing.

Just alignment —

quiet, natural, and exactly on time.

And this is when you begin to understand something powerful:

The life meant for you was never far.

It was simply waiting for you to become the person who could receive it.

PART 4: WALKING AWAY FROM WHAT NO LONGER BELONGS

As you begin aligning with your truth, something becomes clear —

not everything from your past can come with you into your future.

Growth reveals what no longer fits.

It shows you which connections drain you, which habits limit you, which environments suppress you, and which versions of yourself you have finally outgrown.

Walking away is not a rejection of your past.

It is an acceptance of your evolution.

There was a girl named Meera who spent years holding onto friendships that no longer felt supportive. She stayed because of history, shared memories, and the fear of hurting anyone.

But as she grew, she noticed a simple truth:

Her heart felt heavier after every conversation.

One day, she realized something profound —

sometimes letting go is the kindest thing you can do for yourself.

Walking away didn't mean she stopped caring.

It meant she started caring for herself too.

There was a man named Aarav who held on to an identity that no longer reflected who he was. He tried to be who people expected him to be, even though every part of him felt misaligned.

Eventually, he understood that he could no longer carry a version of himself that was built from fear and approval.

He walked away —

not from people,

but from the old version of himself.

Walking away becomes easier when you realize:

- your peace matters
- your growth matters
- your energy matters
- your truth matters
- your future matters
- your heart deserves better

Walking away is not running.

It is choosing alignment.

There was a woman named Zara who stayed in a situationship that constantly left her questioning her worth. She waited for clarity, waited for effort, waited for love — but none of it came.

The day she decided to walk away wasn't dramatic.

It was quiet.

Gentle.

Honest.

It was the moment she finally accepted:

"I can't build my future in a place that keeps breaking me."

Leaving what no longer belongs is not always painful.

Sometimes it is relief disguised as sadness.

Sometimes it is peace disguised as loss.

Sometimes it is respect disguised as distance.

Walking away also includes releasing:

- overthinking
- self-doubt
- guilt for choosing yourself
- the need to explain your worth
- the habit of shrinking to fit
- the pressure to please
- the fear of disappointing others

Letting go is not about removing people or things from your life —

it's about removing the weight they place on your spirit.

There was a boy named Kabir who once said,

"I thought letting go meant losing. But now I know it means returning to myself."

And he was right.

Walking away is a return —

a return to your peace,

your clarity,

your boundaries,

your confidence,

your direction.

When you release what no longer belongs, life finally has space to give you what does.

People arrive who understand your worth.

Opportunities appear that match your growth.

Moments unfold that align with your path.

Walking away is not a step back.

It is the step that allows everything else to move forward.

Because the truth is simple:

You cannot step into the life meant for you

while holding onto what was meant only for your past.

PART 5: STEPPING INTO THE LIFE MEANT FOR YOU

There comes a moment — gentle, quiet, and almost unnoticeable at first — when you realize you are no longer living from fear, old wounds, or confusion.

You are living from clarity.

The life you once felt unprepared for begins to feel like the life you were always meant to grow into.

It doesn't happen suddenly.

It doesn't arrive with fireworks.

It happens in soft shifts:

- you wake up without the heaviness you once carried

- you make decisions without doubting your worth
- you say “no” without guilt
- you protect your peace without apology
- you walk toward opportunities without fear
- you trust your inner voice more than others ’opinions

This is the moment you step into the life meant for you.

There was a woman named Jhanvi who used to second-guess every decision. She felt responsible for everyone else’s comfort and forgot her own.

But as she grew — through regret, clarity, and courage — something changed.

She began choosing what felt true, not what felt safe.

One day she caught herself smiling at nothing in particular.

And that’s when she knew:

she had entered a new chapter of her life.

A chapter where she belonged to herself again.

There was a boy named Soham who always feared taking risks. He believed stability meant staying where he was, even if it drained him.

But slowly, as he listened to his inner direction, he realized that the real risk was abandoning his own calling.

The day he said yes to an opportunity he once thought he didn’t deserve, he took his first step into the future waiting for him.

Stepping into the life meant for you feels like alignment —

a quiet click inside the soul.

It feels like:

- peace replacing old chaos
- strength replacing hesitation
- trust replacing fear
- direction replacing confusion
- self-respect replacing overthinking
- calm replacing urgency

Nothing around you may look different —

but everything inside you does.

The life meant for you isn't perfect.

It's honest.

It's aligned.

It's lived with awareness, not avoidance.

It reflects who you truly are, not who you once pretended to be.

There was a girl named Tara who once lived in constant doubt. Her choices were shaky, her confidence fragile.

But through her journey, she discovered something profound:

The life meant for you doesn't require you to become someone else.

It only requires you to stop abandoning yourself.

This is the true meaning of destiny in your book —

not a scripted plan or a magical certainty,

but a life created from clarity, courage, and self-respect.

You step into the life meant for you when:

- you trust your timing
- you honor your emotions
- you choose people who choose you
- you stop forcing what isn't real
- you believe you are deserving
- you walk in the direction that brings you peace
- you finally feel ready to receive good things

And slowly, life responds.

The right people appear.

The right opportunities flow.

The right moments align.

The right clarity settles inside you.

This isn't luck.

This is you stepping into alignment —

the destination your entire journey has been preparing you for.

You are no longer surviving.

You are living.

You are no longer walking blindly.

You are walking with awareness.

You are no longer carrying your past.

You are carrying your wisdom.

Stepping into the life meant for you doesn't mean everything becomes easy —

it means everything becomes meaningful.

This is the doorway your heart has been walking toward since Chapter 1.

And now, with all the clarity, regret, courage, and transformation behind you:

You are ready.

You are aligned.

You are stepping into the life meant for you —

fully, softly, and consciously.

"God has given us the canvas, and we are the ones who become the printers of it — choosing every color, every stroke, every meaning our life will hold."

REFERENCE LIST

1. Frankl, Viktor E. (2006). *Man's Search for Meaning*. Beacon Press.

2. Tolle, Eckhart. (2004). *The Power of Now*. New World Library.

3. Brown, Brené. (2012). *Daring Greatly*. Avery Publishing.

4. Coelho, Paulo. (1993). *The Alchemist*. HarperOne.

5. Covey, Stephen R. (2013). *The 7 Habits of Highly Effective People*. Simon & Schuster.

6. Clear, James. (2018). *Atomic Habits*. Avery.

7. Gibran, Kahlil. (1923). *The Prophet*. Alfred A. Knopf.

8. Murphy, Joseph. (1963). *The Power of Your Subconscious Mind*. Penguin Random House.

9. Nhat Hanh, Thich. (1998). *The Heart of the Buddha's Teaching*. Broadway Books.

10. Senge, Peter M. (2006). *The Fifth Discipline*. Currency.